BORIS JOHNSON IN 100 FACTS

EUGENE L. WOLFE

AMBERLEY

This book is dedicated to my mother, Mary R. Wolfe, who thought Boris was 'a riot' until she learned some of the facts that follow.

First published 2020

Amberley Publishing
The Hill, Stroud
Gloucestershire, GL5 4EP

www.amberley-books.com

British Library Cataloguing in Publication Data.
A catalogue record for this book is available from the British Library.

ISBN 978 1 3981 0344 3 (paperback)
ISBN 978 1 3981 0345 0 (ebook)

Typeset in 10pt on 12.5pt Sabon.
Typesetting by Aura Technology and Software Services, India.
Printed in the UK.

Contents

1. BORN AN UNLIKELY BREXIT CHAMPION

Although Boris Johnson's intelligence and ability were evident from early on, in many ways his background and childhood were quite poor predictors of the man he would become. Nowhere was the contrast as stark as in his politics.

The virtual embodiment of European unity makes a rather unlikely future champion of Brexit. The BBC genealogy programme *Who Do You Think You Are?* found that Johnson was related not only to the British Royal Family, by way of direct descent from George II, but also to those of Sweden, the Netherlands and Russia. He also is the great-grandson of Ali Kemal, a journalist and Ottoman politician who was murdered for opposing the Nationalist movement led by Kemal Atatürk. Reflecting on his ancestry, Johnson observed, 'It is interesting to observe how British I can feel and yet, actually, what a complete mongrel composition I really am.'[1] Not long before, while campaigning (successfully) to become Mayor of London, Johnson had described himself (incorrectly) as the grandson of a Muslim immigrant from Turkey before going on to indicate his support for an amnesty for those who had come to Britain illegally, a stance at odds with his own party's policy.[2] He had also been a passionate advocate of Turkey's entry into the EU. So, it was surprising not only that a man with such a background would argue that Britain should leave Europe but do so by claiming (dubiously) that if it did not, the country would be inundated by millions of Turks.[3]

The stereotypical Brexiteer is a Little Englander who neither knows nor cares much about the world beyond the borders of Albion. Boris hardly fits that mould. Alexander Boris de Pfeffel Johnson was born in New York City on 19 June 1964. Over the

---

1 'Mayor of London Boris Johnson is a distant relative of the Queen,' by Anita Singh, 4 August 2008, telegraph.co.uk.

2 Purnell, Sonia, *Just Boris: A Tale of Blond Ambition* (London: Aurum, 2012), p. 340.

3 Gimson, Andrew, *Boris: The Making of the Prime Minister* (London: Simon & Schuster, 2016), p. 7.

next 14 years he, with his mother Charlotte (née Fawcett), father Stanley and growing band of siblings, Rachel (born 1965), Leo (1967) and Joseph (1971) moved 32 times. The family would bounce between the US, England and Belgium, where Stanley would become one of the first British officials to work for the European Commission. Yet even familiarity with the stifling dreariness of 1970s Brussels hardly bred in young Boris contempt for the EU. On the contrary, when a 2016 referendum was called on Britain's continued membership in Europe, he agonised for days over which side to support.[4]

If Boris's background and childhood did not inevitably create a Brexiteer, they did have a formative effect. At 10 Boris was sent to Ashdown House, a preparatory boarding school in East Sussex, where he apparently was teased for his Turkish lineage and time spent abroad. In response, Boris, who already was quite familiar with P. G. Wodehouse, created, in the words of a family friend, 'a dishevelled look and persona, this 1930s-style English eccentric who appears to be bumbling, but is actually fantastically well read. It was a survival tactic and it worked brilliantly.' The experience also fostered, in the words of a biographer, 'a genuine empathy for outsiders' that would become 'an important element of his popular appeal'.[5]

If adult Boris would eventually use this contrived persona to create a larger-than-life public personality, this too was quite unexpected to those who knew him as a youth. Afflicted with severe deafness until about eight, Boris was 'a subdued, reflective small child'. Family friends remember him as quiet and studious, often with his nose in a book. 'Photos during this period regularly show Boris as a serious, even solemn young boy, not the cheeky little rogue one might expect.'[6]

The roguish elements of Boris's adult personality seem largely attributable to his father. As an April Fool's joke in 1968, Stanley applied to the World Bank, then his employer, for a $100 million loan to build three pyramids and a sphinx

---

4 ibid., p. xi.
5 Purnell, p. 42.
6 ibid., p. 14.

in Egypt to promote tourism. Soon thereafter he was in search of a job. But Stanley had some less-endearing qualities. When Charlotte was about to give birth to Boris, Stanley – who did not believe 'real men bothered' with the 'horrific details' of parturition – stepped out for a pizza until the deed was done. Thereafter, he was frequently absent from the family for long periods.

This, plus his repeated infidelity, contributed to Charlotte's 1974 nervous breakdown, which resulted in long-term hospitalisation. Some have attributed 'the flamboyance, deliberate cheerfulness and resilience' of Boris and his siblings to the extended absence of their beloved mother. But it is also evident that Boris was 'greatly affected' by his father's philandering, his mother's depression, and the pair's eventual divorce.[7] So it is perhaps not surprising that adult Boris 'is in many ways a homely man, who after a meeting in some distant town prefers to drive back through the night to his wife and children than stay alone in a hotel.'[8] Less expected is that, in terms of marital fidelity, this particular apple does not fall farther from the paternal tree.

---

7 ibid., pp. 6, 10, 16, 34.
8 Gimson, p. 176.

2. BORIS IS AN OLD ETONIAN

Johnson arrived at Eton in late 1977 as a King's Scholar, meaning he paid reduced tuition based on academic merit. He later described himself at the time as 'extremely spotty, extremely nerdy, and terribly swotty'. Perhaps as a result, he began to call himself Boris, rather than Alex, abandoned his mother's Catholicism to become an Anglican, and cultivated the eccentric persona that would become his trademark. He soon became both popular and well known, as signified by his election to the Eton Society, or Pop, an elite cadre of senior boys.[1]

Although school reports criticised him for idleness, tardiness, and complacency, Johnson did not lack accomplishments at Eton. He was head boy.[2] He won prizes in both English and Classics, and became secretary of the debating society and editor of the school newspaper.[3] This record did not hurt his already substantial ego. As a childhood acquaintance later observed, 'I was brought up with generations of arrogant Etonian boys but Boris's arrogance transcends any I've ever met. He is the ultimate Etonian product, an opportunist to the core.'[4]

British schoolboys were told that the Battle of Waterloo was won on the playing fields of Eton, a claim based on a misquotation of the Duke of Wellington, who had some experience in both locations. The same certainly seemed true of the political battlefield: twenty prime ministers were Old Etonians, far surpassing the total of Harrow, the school's nearest rival.[5] Indeed, only one prime minister between 1868 and 1905, Benjamin Disraeli, was not an Old Etonian.

---

1 Purnell, pp. 42–9, 55.
2 *The Times*, 30 September 2006, p. 37.
3 Purnell, pp. 49–55.
4 ibid., p. 44.
5 Douglas Hurd was happy to rub this in when he was invited to speak at an annual celebration of Old Harrovians. Spying only seven names on the programme's list of alumni who had reached the apex of the political world, he 'commented that it must be convenient for Harrow to be able to print all its prime ministers on one page. This very Etonian remark was received with hisses.' Hurd, Douglas, *Robert Peel* (London: Phoenix, 2007), p. 9 (f).

Yet the prestige of an Etonian pedigree at the end of the twentieth century was not quite what it had been. The 1956 Suez Crisis, perhaps more than any other event, put paid to the notion that the gentlemen who had attended public schools had a right and duty to rule. When Egyptian leader Gamal Abdel Nasser outmanoeuvred and humiliated Prime Minister Anthony Eden and his cabinet composed exclusively of public school alumni, it helped undermine the deference that had enabled the old elite to dominate politics.[6] Although Eden's two immediate successors, Harold Macmillan and Alec Douglas-Home, would be fellow Old Etonians, it would be more than four decades before another of the school's alumni entered 10 Downing Street. And when that happened, an Old Etonian Prime Minister, David Cameron, would find his tenure cut short in large part due to the efforts of fellow alumnus Boris Johnson. If Eton's playing fields did not produce victory at Waterloo, the school did educate the two men perhaps most responsible for Brexit two centuries later.

6 Marquand, David, *Britain since 1918*, (London: Phoenix, 2008), pp. 163–4.

3. BORIS TOOK A GAP YEAR IN AUSTRALIA

After leaving Eton but before heading off to Oxford Johnson took a gap year, teaching English and Latin at Australia's Geelong Grammar School, which educated the offspring of the wealthiest and most eminent families in Australia and New Zealand (for around £18,000 per year). Boris was assigned to the school's famous Timbertop campus, where Year Nine boys and girls took on an outward-bound course in the foothills of the Great Dividing Range. Life in the wilderness setting, more than a mile from the nearest road, was fairly spartan: television and alcohol were forbidden; phone use was restricted, and if enough wood was not collected for the heaters, students and teachers alike suffered the cold. 'It was a fairly tough regime designed to put backbone into the Antipodean ruling class.' Boris, of course, made an impression, partly because he was the only non-Australian assistant on campus. The school's magazine expected the person it referred to as both Boris and Alexander to be 'remembered for his inimitably stolid style of tractor-driving'.[1]

Boris later recalled, 'I had to deal with these very, very alarming adolescents of both sexes who were extremely difficult to control.' He did not always manage it. One former pupil remembers the young student teacher as not particularly outgoing. 'He was a bit of a dag if you know what I mean. He didn't command a room or anything like that.' She continued, 'I do remember him going red in the face and yelling sometimes so I'm sure we got under his skin a bit.' But what really stood about Boris was 'that mop of hair'.[2]

---

1 Purnell, pp. 58–9.
2 '"He was a bit of a dag": Backpacker Boris taught murderball and Latin,' by Tom Cowie, 26 July 2019, smh.com.au.

4. BORIS STUDIED CLASSICS AT OXFORD

Boris arrived at Oxford in late 1983, having won a scholarship to Balliol College to read Classics. 'While much of Britain languished in post-recession gloom with three million people on the dole, at Oxford the air fizzed with future potential.' Johnson's contemporaries included many who expected to, and did, assume leading positions in politics and the media. As he later would recall, 'What a sharp-elbowed, thrusting and basically repellent lot we were. We were always bragging and shafting each other, and in a way we still are, with our pompous memoirs and calculated indiscretions.'[1]

Boris yearned, 'with a passion barely conceivable to some of us, to take a first-class degree'. Martin Hammond, who had taught Johnson at Eton, felt that his former pupil clearly had the ability to achieve such a result. However, in a letter to Stanley Johnson, Hammond wrote, 'My fear is that Boris may take his easy-going ways with him to Balliol, and add to the damaging statistics of Etonians who do little work at Oxbridge.' Such fears were amply justified, because, for most of his time at Oxford, 'Boris did virtually no academic work'. As Jonathan Barnes, a tutor, would recall, 'If you're intelligent enough, you can rub along in philosophy on a couple of hours a week. Boris rubbed along on no hours a week, and it wasn't quite good enough.' The problem seems less that Boris did not care about his subjects than he had many other things on his mind and, not for the last time, was spread too thinly.[2]

In addition to seeking a wife and joining both the Bullingdon Club and the Oxford Union (hereafter each the subject of separate Facts), Boris played prop forward for four years in the Balliol rugby squad. He also co-edited, with fellow Old Etonian and good friend Darius Guppy, *Tributary*, the university's satirical magazine. This does not seem to have been a great fit because Boris, unwilling to make enemies, did not engage

1 Purnell, p. 62.
2 Gimson, pp. 55, 57, 61–2.

in the ruthless character assassination that was a staple of Oxford's version of *Private Eye*. His editorial successors were less restrained. He took no notice when they called him 'an exiled Armenian chicken farmer' and 'an Aryan bull pig', but when they referred to Johnson as 'incompetent,' at a time he was seeking the presidency of the Oxford Union, Boris stormed into an editor's house at 3 a.m., 'absolutely incandescent' with rage, grabbed a typewriter and tried to re-write the story.[3]

Given his other interests, it is perhaps surprising that Boris almost ended up with a first-class degree. According to Barnes, 'You don't get a First on intelligence alone – you also need to work like stink; he miscalculated slightly and left things too late.' Boris ended up with an upper second-class degree, an 'undoubtedly bitter disappointment ... which lost him sleep then and still rankles to this day.'[4]

3 ibid., pp. 62, 74–5.
4 Purnell, pp. 89, 92.

5. BORIS WAS A MEMBER OF THE NOTORIOUS BULLINGDON CLUB

Founded in 1780, the exclusive all-male dining club at Oxford University was originally dedicated to cricket and horse racing. Before long, however, Bullingdon Club, the membership of which was composed mostly of wealthy former public school boys, gained a reputation for debauchery and destruction. So much so that the Prince of Wales was able to persuade his parents to let him join in 1913 only on the condition that he not attend any 'Bullingdon blinds', the notoriously raucous club dinners. When word reached Queen Mary that her son had, in fact, done so, he was instructed to resign his membership.[1] A little more than a decade later, Bullingdon members, 'armed with hockey sticks, copper kettles, pieces of coal and other things invaded the quadrangles at Christ Church and bombarded windows, with the result that more than five hundred panes of glass were broken'.[2] This incident led to the club being banned from meeting within 15 miles of Oxford.

In the mid-1980s female prostitutes performed sex acts at Club dinners that featured extensive drinking and destruction, as well as the belittling of women and the intimidation of those less posh. A woman who acted as a potential scout for new members later recalled of Johnson, 'Boris was one of the big beasts of the club. He was up for anything. They treated certain types of people with absolute disdain, and referred to them as "plebs" or "grockles", and the police were always called "plod". Their attitude was that women were there for their entertainment.'[3]

Although another contemporary recalled that Boris 'did not attend frequently and held reservations about the wildest alcohol-fuelled antics', Johnson was involved in a notorious incident in which he and fellow member David Cameron managed to elude police after vandalising a restaurant in 1987

---

1 *The New York Times*, 28 May 1913, p. 1.
2 *The New York Times*, 23 February 1927, p. 3.
3 'Sexism, Vandalism and Bullying: Inside the Boris Johnson-era Bullingdon Club', Harriet Sherwood, 7 July 2019, Theguardian.com.

by hiding in shrubbery. 'Boris claims he was one of those locked up overnight, before being released without charge. Others, who were incarcerated, insist he is merely trying to play up his prankster past and he was never in fact held in custody.'[4]

For years afterward, Boris embraced his past, attending Bullingdon events and greeting former members with a shout of 'Buller, Buller, Buller'. Then, like Cameron (and two other Bullingdonians who would go on to attain ministerial positions, George Osborne and Jo Johnson) Boris sought to distance himself from his Bullingdon days, calling an infamous photograph of him and other Club members, 'a truly shameful vignette of almost superhuman undergraduate arrogance, toffishness and twittishness'.[5]

Since Boris's departure, however, the club has put on a garden party, 'invited a string band to play and proceeded to destroy all the instruments, including a Stradivarius'. In 2005, four Bullingdon members, including Alexander Fellowes, nephew of Princess Diana, spent a night in jail after a brawl in a fifteenth-century pub. Although, as usual, the 'Bullers' paid cash for their damage, and left a healthy tip, this did not prevent the proprietor from calling the police, a reaction described by one member as 'unfair'.[6]

Boris's apparent re-evaluation of his undergraduate antics helps explain why people reportedly have been turning down Bullingdon membership in recent years, so much so that in 2016 the Club was said to be on the brink of closure. Two years later, the Oxford University Conservative Association banned members of the Club from its ranks, arguing that such individuals 'have no place in the modern party', a comment hard to square with two recent Bullingdonian residents of 10 Downing Street.[7]

---

4 Purnell, p. 64.
5 'Boris, Dave and George: The Power of Networking,' thehistorycollection.co.
6 'Smashing Jobs Chaps: Exclusive Inside Look at Bullingdon Club,' by Sophie McBain, 6 August 2009, theoxfordstudent.com.
7 'The Bullingdon is on its uppers. Let's all celebrate by trashing a restaurant.' By Barbara Ellen, 14 October 2018, theguardian.com.

6. BORIS WAS ELECTED PRESIDENT OF THE OXFORD UNION

One of Johnson's main goals of his university years was to become president of the prestigious Oxford Union, a debating society institutionally independent from the University, even if a majority of its members are students. It was at the Union that 'Boris the would-be politician refined his oratory, and the no less necessary crafts of intrigue and deceit.' As he later explained, success in Union elections required 'a disciplined and deluded collection of stooges' who would canvass for votes in their colleges. The acquisition of stooges is founded on 'duplicity' since the candidate for senior office cannot possibly fulfil a promise to do as much to help all of them achieve junior office as they do to help him. According to Johnson, 'The terrible art of the candidate is to coddle the self-deception of the stooge.' One of the stooges Boris managed to recruit was Michael Gove, who would later join him on the Tory benches in the Commons.[1]

In 1984 an apparently overconfident Johnson was defeated in the presidency election by Neil Sherlock in 'a titanic and ill-tempered contest that strayed dangerously into class warfare'. Two years later, Boris tried again. This time he made more effective use of his stooges. He also sought to expand his support beyond the upper classes in general and Old Etonians with whom he tended to socialise in particular. Playing down his Conservative sympathies, Boris sought to become 'a politically androgynous personality, seemingly offering something for everyone'. By affecting sympathy for, and by some accounts even joining, the trendy Social Democratic Party, Boris managed to capture the Union presidency.[2]

1 Gimson, pp. 68–70.
2 Purnell, pp. 71, 81–2.

7. BORIS MARRIED ALLEGRA MOSTYN-OWEN IN 1987

Another of Johnson's main ambitions upon arriving at Oxford in late 1983 was to find a wife. That might not have been a goal expected of someone who, a year earlier, had written on his page of the Eton College Leaving Book of his intention to pursue 'more notches on my phallocratic phallus'. But as biographer Andrew Gimson observers, 'There is kind of ambitious man who wants to get married just in order to have his private life settled, so he can get on with the serious business of his career. Boris's urge to marry so young seems more likely to be a sign of his desire to emulate his father's achievements. He may also have wanted to create new and intact family.'[1]

Allegra Mostyn-Owen, aristocratic, intelligent and beautiful, was thought to be 'the most desired girl in Oxford of her time'. That her face had appeared on the cover of *Tatler* magazine and billboards around Oxford 'merely served to make her appear even more elevated and untouchable – except to the super-confident or the terribly deluded'. She did not lack posh beaus. 'Bagging this most glorious prize against such intense competition – particularly since he was neither rich nor landed ... raised Boris's university status considerably.'[2]

Johnson 'bagged' his quarry in typical bumbling fashion: by showing up with a bottle of wine at her room the day before she was to throw a party there. They drank, had a nice chat, and he made her laugh. Soon they were dining out together, though Allegra was not entirely sure whether he wanted to be more than just friends. Eventually he persuaded her to date him by saying that if she did not consent, he could not continue to spend so much time with her but instead would focus on other things.

1 Gimson, pp. 55–6.
2 Purnell, p. 72.

'Now dependent on her ambitious young suitor, she agreed, allowing Boris to start calling the shots.'[3]

By late 1985, Boris and Allegra were discussing marriage. Specifically, he sent her a letter asking if she had broached the subject with her parents, who 'were appalled by Boris'. Her father considered him 'rapacious'. Her elegant mother was horrified by his 'wilfully scruffy manner'. It did not help that, when he joined the family for a skiing holiday, he forgot his passport and had to take a later flight. When he finally did arrive, he discovered that his suitcase contained only dirty sheets. 'Boris went skiing in his normal clothes, a tweed jacket and moleskin trousers, and liked going very fast straight downhill.' Such apparent disorganisation, feigned or otherwise, may not have endeared Boris to Allegra's parents, but, typically, it led her to take pity on him by doing all his laundry while at university.[4]

Such issues notwithstanding, the couple finally married on 5 September 1987. The ceremony was lovely, but the omens were not. Within an hour, Boris had lost his wedding ring. Given that he had made clear he was not keen to wear it (partly, it seems, because his father never did) it seems possible that the ring's disappearance was not completely inadvert. To make matters worse, Boris arrived at his wedding without the required attire. And he then proceeded to misplace the wedding certificate, which turned up months later in the trousers he had borrowed for his nuptials. As Gimson observes with some understatement, 'This is not the behaviour of a man who is going to be very solicitous of his wife's feelings.'[5]

---

3 ibid., pp. 74–5.
4 Gimson, pp. 81–2.
5 ibid., p. 86.

8. BORIS WAS FIRED FROM *THE TIMES* FOR INVENTING A QUOTE

Following university graduation, and a very brief stint as a management consultant, Johnson used family connections to secure a job as graduate trainee at *The Times* in late 1987. He was not without relevant background, having served as editor of *The Eton College Chronicle* and co-editor of *Tributary*, Oxford University's satirical magazine.[1]

The first *Times* article under the Boris Johnson by-line came out in April 1988. It detailed the frustration of those seeking to claim benefits shortly before eligibility rules changed.[2] Unsurprisingly, many of the 31 articles he would write for the newspaper were on topics with which he had at least some familiarity. The former president of the Oxford Union reported on an inquiry into the National Union of Students.[3] The former resident of Belgium was sent back to that country to write about a ferry strike.[4] The Classics scholar considered claims that a sculpture thought to be a masterpiece from fifth-century BC Greece might actually be a fake from the Victorian era.[5]

Johnson's work at *The Times* provide some of the first public displays of his signature wit. An article on the discoveries of an expedition to Tibet, including 'a collection of not easily explicable faeces', is entitled 'Yeti hunters show a pile of evidence.'[6] (OK, it ain't Oscar Wilde.) But his tenure at *The Times* also revealed a less admirable trait, one that would cause problems in the short term but pay dividends later on.

In late May 1988 Johnson wrote his first page-one story, on the discovery by archaeologists of King Edward II's 'Rosary' Palace on the South Bank of the Thames in London. The article contained the indirect quotation, 'According to Dr Colin Lucas,

---

1 Purnell, pp. 49, 53, 68, 94–9.
2 *The Times*, 9 April 1988, p. 2.
3 *The Times*, 21 April 1988, p. 5.
4 *The Times*, 2 May 1988, p. 3.
5 *The Times*, 28 April 1988, p. 7.
6 *The Times*, 9 June 1988, p. 4.

of Balliol College, Oxford, this is where the king enjoyed a reign of dissolution with his catamite, Piers Gaveston, before he was gruesomely murdered at Berkeley Castle by barons who felt the was too prone to foreign influence.'[7] But four days later, in article on how the discovery of timber supports may allow a more accurate determination of the date of the palace's construction, Johnson seems to backtrack. After indicating that the only documentary evidence dates the palace to 1325, two years before the king's murder, Johnson quotes Lucas as saying 'Edward II is reputed to have led a life of wine and song with his catamite Piers Gaveston. But if 1325 is correct, that could hardly have taken place in this building since Gaveston was executed in 1312.'[8]

Lucas, an expert on Revolutionary France, might have been mildly embarrassed by his apparent confusion about the reign of Edward II. It turns out he was one of the first victims of a recorded Boris falsehood, for Johnson had made up the quote that he attributed to his godfather. When the editor of *The Times* discovered the deception, Johnson was sacked.[9]

---

7 *The Times*, 20 May 1988, p. 1.
8 *The Times*, 24 May 1988, p. 4.
9 Purnell, pp. 100–2.

9. BORIS WAS HIRED BY *THE DAILY TELEGRAPH*

Not long after being fired by the *Times*, Boris was hired by the newspaper's arch-rival, the *Daily Telegraph*. This rather impressive feat owed much to Johnson's networking skills. As President of the Oxford Union, Boris had invited Max Hastings to a debate. The former war correspondent who recently had become editor of the *Telegraph* later recalled being struck less by Johnson's academic background than by his ability to stand out in a crowd: 'I realised that this callow white lump in formal evening dress was a lot better at playing an audience than I was.' So when Boris later asked for a job, Hastings put him on the public-schoolboy-dominated leader-writing desk. Not for the first or last time, Johnson lucked out. No longer the star graduate with an unblemished record, without Hastings' patronage, it is quite possible that Boris would have been lost to journalism forever at this point.[1]

Boris and the *Telegraph* proved a good fit. He began to develop a personal writing style, 'using gloriously old-fashioned phrases, words and humour that set him apart from the other, more earnest young men at the leader writers' desk. His copy was fun to read; it literally sounded good.' He often said the opposite of what he meant while making that clear to the reader, 'a clever device that takes the confrontational sting out of controversial opinions while at the same time appearing amusingly self-mocking'. And he built rapport with readers by addressing them as 'my friends' or '*mes amis*'. In short, 'Boris appealed brilliantly to the "country's going to the dogs" traditionalist instincts of the middle-class, middle-aged, middle-England readership of the *Telegraph*.'[2]

BORIS JOHNSON IN 100 FACTS

---

1 ibid., pp. 102–3.
2 ibid., pp. 106–8.

10. *THE TELEGRAPH* SENT BORIS TO BRUSSELS

Such was Boris's success writing leaders for the *Telegraph* that when a vacancy arose in the paper's Brussels bureau in early 1989, the man who had spent part of his childhood in the city and spoke not only good French and Italian but passable Spanish and German was the obvious candidate. Although he knew, through his father, many of the key players in the EU personally, Boris had little experience of news reporting. At first he seemed out of his depth but, by cultivating a bumbling image and doling out heaps of flattery, Boris often won the assistance of established Brussels hands. But soon he realised that he did not need to play their game. 'Boris's genius lay in recognising that Brussels reporting had become a cosy cartel, in which the various correspondents produced broadly sympathetic accounts of the EU's activities. He spotted a commercial opportunity – the chance to make his name by doing what he does best: being different.'[1]

But that was not all he did. Back in mid-1986 Boris had helped Allegra write an article that appeared under her name in the *Sunday Telegraph*. It later caused her 'deep embarrassment' when it was revealed that an important detail had been omitted. This was seen to mark the emergence of what would become a distinctive element of Johnson's journalism: 'the powerful and amusing article, utterly convincing in its general drift, but weakened by cavalier treatment of mere facts.'[2]

Johnson made a name for himself, and fanned Euroscepticism not only in Britain but throughout the EU, by writing humorous stories about the antics of bureaucrats in Brussels that were not exactly true. Among the 'Euromyths' he peddled were purported plans to introduce one-size 'eurocoffins', to establish a 'banana police force' to regulate the shape of the fruit,

---

1 ibid., pp. 109, 112, 114.
2 Gimson, p. 83.

and to ban prawn cocktail crisps.[3] Eurocrats were portrayed as 'rejecting new specifications for condom dimensions', to the dismay of Italian manufacturers who sought a smaller minimum width, an account an official later dismissed as 'a load of bullshit'. There were articles on a (non-existent) EU plan to erect the world's tallest building for its headquarters, or to blow up Berlaymont, the European commission's existing asbestos-riddled headquarters. Of the latter, a former colleague observed, 'It was a great story, but it was complete bollocks.' And that was the thing. Boris was not the first British journalist to look at the EU with a sceptical eye, but he did so in such a witty and entertaining manner that other reporters faced pressure to follow suit, even if Johnson's claims were not entirely accurate. As former *Times* correspondent Peter Guilford recalls, 'there was this sort of Eurosceptic-generating machine that we were all part of, and Boris was driving harder than anyone else.'[4]

To Boris obviously does not belong all the credit or blame for the Eurosceptic tide that began to roll over Britain while he was at EU headquarters. Half a year before his arrival Prime Minister Margaret Thatcher effectively had declared war on the 'European super state'. Still, 'so powerful did Boris become while still in his 20s that some visiting Ministers of the Crown would delay press conferences until he deigned to turn up (while others fearing his difficult questioning would secretly pray he would not show up at all). Virtually all would spend hours deliberating on how to 'Boris-proof' their policies or announcements.'[5]

3 'Boris Johnson: the most infamous lies and untruths by the Conservative leadership candidate,' by Peter Stubley, 24 May 2019, independent.co.uk.
4 'How Boris Johnson's Brussels-bashing stories shaped British politics,' by Jennifer Rankin and Jim Waterson, 14 July 2019, theguardian.com.
5 Purnell, p 117.

11. BORIS MARRIED MARINA WHEELER IN 1993

No long after his marriage, Boris began the ardent pursuit of a career, a mistress he would chase with at least as much passion as he had wooed Allegra. Indeed, disdaining advice to treat his young wife 'like porcelain', he instead left her to gather dust like an old clay pot as he followed newspaper stories. Allegra later would lament, 'When we got married it was the end of the relationship, instead of the beginning.' Things only got worse in 1989, when Boris became the Brussels correspondent for the *Telegraph*. Frequently absent, Johnson paid little attention to Allegra, who was desperate for emotional support amid the breakdown of her parents' marriage.[1]

According to biographer Andrew Gimson, 'Boris is a humane man, in the sense that he feels things deeply, and this emotional warmth has always drawn people to him and has saved his jokes from ringing hollow. People sense there is a suffering man behind the comic act. But he could also be quite staggeringly inconsiderate.' In Brussels this meant that he frequently flew off in pursuit of a story without bothering to tell Allegra where he had gone. On occasion, she had to ring the *Telegraph*'s foreign desk to find out where her husband was. Then, to add insult to injury, he would later castigate her for the ribbing from colleagues that ensued. By February 1990, fearing that she was headed for the same sort of nervous breakdown suffered by Boris's mother, Allegra left. Both she and Boris were devastated, but they began divorce proceedings. Then there was a reconciliation.[2]

While Allegra worked on trying to save her marriage, Boris, never one to be alone for long, began to revive an old friendship. He had known Marina Wheeler since childhood. They had been schoolmates in Brussels, a period in which his enthusiasm for her company had not been reciprocated. But as fate would have it, she returned to the Belgian capital in 1990

1 ibid., pp. 98, 109–10.
2 Gimson, pp. 108–10.

to work for a British law firm. 'Despairing of his marriage, Boris pursued Marina devotedly, bombarding her with phone calls and flattery.'[3] This was not at first welcome. Marina resisted, but this only intensified his pursuit. 'She remembers crying with frustration that he would not go away.'[4]

Allegra, splitting her time between Brussels and London, where she was studying, inadvertently fanned the flames by frequently inviting Marina over for dinner, taking pity on Boris's friend who lived in 'crappy digs'. Marina and her family insist that her romantic involvement with Boris did not begin until after his relationship with Allegra ended. Others are not so sure. In any event, as it became clear that Boris saw Marina as more than just a friend, his relationship with Allegra became increasingly 'acrimonious'.[5]

At one point, following 'a row that got out of hand', Allegra reportedly sought refuge in the flat of friend Louisa Gosling, 'looking shocked, scared and on the brink of tears' and making a 'serious allegation' about Boris's conduct and his frightening temper.[6]

Finally, in early 1992, Allegra departed for good, taking all the furniture with her. 'Marina helped Boris refurnish his home – and rebuild his life. And then she moved in.'[7]

In October 1992 Marina became pregnant. Allegra graciously agreed to an expedited divorce. 'Boris was a bachelor for twelve days. His divorce came through on 26 April 1993 and on 8 May he married Marina at Horsham town hall in Sussex, near her parent's home.'[8]

---

3 Purnell, p. 131.
4 Gimson, p. 111.
5 Purnell, pp. 131–2.
6 "'I'm still scared of Boris' Pal of Boris Johnson's first wife claims he grabbed and threatened her 30 years ago over claims about couple's private life," by Phoebe Cooke, 30 June 2019, thesun.co.uk.
7 Purnell, p. 132.
8 Gimson, pp. 113–4.

12. BORIS TRIED TO HELP A FRIEND ASSAULT A NOSY JOURNALIST

Darius Guppy, the scion of a prominent Iranian family, became close friends with Johnson at Eton. They later attended Oxford together, where both were members of the Bullingdon Club. In 1990 Guppy called Johnson with a request for help.

Angry at a scandal involving Lloyd's of London that had ruined his father financially, Guppy had sought revenge. He hired someone to stage a fake robbery and to tie up Guppy and a friend in a New York hotel and shoot a mattress for effect. When the police came, Guppy convinced them that he had been subject to a jewel heist. Lloyd's paid him £1.8 million in compensation for the 'stolen' valuables.

But there was a problem. The 'robber,' Peter Risdon, was upset with his pay-out. And *News of the World* journalist Stuart Collier was beginning to ask questions. Guppy wanted to have Collier assaulted as a warning, so he called Johnson for help, not realising that Risdon was secretly recording the conversation.

On the tape, released almost two decades later, Guppy states that he has arranged for someone to attack Collier, but cannot find the journalist's address. Johnson indicated that he had tried to help, approaching four people in an effort to get the information, but was very worried that he could be tied to the attack. Boris also wanted assurances that Collier would not be seriously injured. Guppy promised that the journalist would not have to go to intensive care but would only receive a couple black eyes and maybe a cracked rib, the same sorts of injuries Johnson had sustained playing rugby.[1]

Although Johnson apparently never provided Collier's address, Guppy had reason to worry. In early 1993 he was sent

1 'Darius, Boris and a blast from the past,' by Andy McSmith, 31 March 2009, independent.co.uk.

to prison for five years for insurance fraud stemming from the fake robbery.[2] A month later he pleaded guilty in court to three charges relating to false claims of almost £200,000 VAT on purported exports of gold bullion to Switzerland.[3]

The sordid tale does not end there. After the recording was made public, BBC journalist Eddie Mair called Johnson, by now Mayor of London, 'a nasty piece of work'. Guppy, angry at the treatment of his friend, wrote an article for the *New Statesman*, 'Who will bully the bullies?' In it, he recounted that, in response to a journalist's insult to his wife, Guppy had tracked down the individual's address, flown to London from his home in South Africa, and gone to the man's residence. When the journalist emerged, Guppy chased him, knocked him down and 'emptied over his head a sack of horse manure rendered slurry by the addition of bottled water'. Although he humiliated the man in front of his wife and his neighbours, who came outside at the sound of screaming, Guppy indicated that he had resisted the ultimate mortification: a video of the attack, filmed by two accomplices, was not put online.[4] Still, journalists who might criticize Boris had been warned.

---

2 '"I knocked him to the ground and tipped slurry on his head": Boris Johnson's friend Darius Guppy admits to horrifying attack on journalist "who insulted his wife",' 12 July 2013, dailymail.co.uk

3 'Guppy spun web of deceit in bullion fraud,' 4 March 1993, heraldscotland.com.

4 'Who will bully the bullies?' by Darius Guppy, 11 July 2013, newstatesman.com

13. BORIS BECAME A TELEVISION STAR

Johnson appeared only a handful of times on *Have I Got News for You*, but the BBC programme turned him into a television star. His success was all the more remarkable because his first visit was so painful. It was customary for panellists to spring nasty surprises on guests, and this Ian Hislop, editor of *Private Eye*, did by dredging up a recording on which Johnson appears to agree to help his friend, Darius Guppy, find the address of a journalist Guppy wants assaulted (Fact 12). Boris was livid about being led into 'an elephant trap', later writing in *The Spectator* that he had been 'stitched up' by the hosts of a show that was 'a fraud' because the apparent 'lightning repartee' actually was the result of meticulous preparation, careful scripting and extensive editing. This might have ended his association with the programme, but he soon made peace and was invited back. He then made light of the article and did not deny Hislop's suggestion that he might have been inebriated when he wrote it. 'Hislop felt disarmed by Boris's willingness to admit to virtually any charge made against him.' In a later edition, he was unable to answer any questions about Iain Duncan Smith, his party leader. 'Audiences loved such towering ineptitude. With many contestants, such behaviour might have become embarrassing, but Boris knew how to carry it off. He was tough enough to take the knocks, and the worse things went for him, the more he could make people laugh.'[1]

Johnson's seven appearances on the programme brought him to the attention of millions who did not read *The Telegraph* or *The Spectator*. They helped turn an Old Etonian into a man of the people and seemed at least partially to expiate some of his more notorious transgressions. 'No one could believe that this jolly fellow could have been caught up in anything sinister involving professional beatings and cracked ribs. He may have come over as a 1930s upper-class twit, but he was box office. He lapped it up – and the TV bosses did, too.'

1 Gimson, pp. 127–8.

That he intentionally mussed his hair before the cameras rolled did not matter. 'It was an act, but a brilliant one.' Appearances on other TV shows – *Parkinson, Breakfast with Frost, Question Time* and *Top Gear* – soon followed.[2]

In hindsight, some complained that it was the country that got played. The show made stars of politicians who would use their celebrity to beguile voters into supporting disastrous policies, such as Brexit. Writing in *The Guardian*, Stuart Heritage argued, 'Boris Johnson's entire buffoonish eye-rolling Oh-Boris smokescreen of a persona was forged in the fires' of his seven appearances on the programme between 1998 and 2006. And Jacob Rees-Mogg, another champion of Brexit, used his appearances to gain 'a reputation as a harmless, self-deprecating Victorian caricature, only unveiling his true dark form once we'd been lulled into a false sense of security.'[3] Hislop himself dismissed the notion that *Have I Got News for You* had fuelled Johnson's rise, arguing that the panellists had never treated him gently. Still, he admitted, 'There is a sense of guilt that part of Boris's success has been built on his performances' on the programme.[4]

2 Purnell, pp.177–8.
3 'The one positive of Brexit? It might make *Have I Got News for You* watchable again,' by Stuart Heritage, 5 April 2019, theguardian.com.
4 *The New York Times*, 30 October 2019, pp. C1 and C6.

14. BORIS LOST HIS FIRST PARLIAMENTARY ELECTION

As Johnson's star rose, his political ambitions became more obvious. From 1993 he sought to become a Tory candidate in elections to the European Parliament. This was not welcomed by many in the party with more positive views of Europe, including Prime Minister John Major. 'The thought of Boris, the notorious scourge of federalist and Europhiles everywhere, staking rightful claim to the Parliamentary palaces of Brussels, Strasbourg and Luxembourg was, for some, too much to bear.'[1]

Boris next pursued a seat in Westminster. As often the case for aspiring MPs, this meant taking on something of a lost cause. His attempt to become Conservative candidate for the London constituency of Holborn and St Pancras, held by Labour since its creation in 1983, was rejected because of a 'badly typed' CV. He then managed to win selection for Clwyd South in North Wales, even though 'his hand-written application letter arrived late, was barely legible and did not include a CV.' A word from the Conservative Central Office, apparently keen to promote (or perhaps more accurately, test) a would-be star, evidently helped.[2]

Winning this safe Labour seat was never really an option, but Boris gave it a go. 'He learned to sing the Welsh national anthem and to order fish and chips in Welsh.'[3] He spent six weeks campaigning in the constituency, studying the intricacies of farm policy. 'His willingness to learn and his ability to get on with people from all walks of life won him many admirers locally, even among non-Tories.'[4] In the end, the tides against him were simply too strong to overcome. He lost to Labour rival Martyn Jones by a more than 2:1 margin.

---

1 Purnell, pp. 162–4.
2 ibid., p. 185.
3 Gimson, p. 125.
4 Purnell, p. 186.

15. BORIS WAS APPOINTED EDITOR OF *THE SPECTATOR* IN 1999

In July 1999 Boris Johnson was appointed editor of *The Spectator*, a right-wing magazine for which he long had written a regular column. Under Frank Johnson (no relation), the man Boris replaced, *The Spectator*, though 'profitable and enjoying a healthy circulation of 57,000, was generally thought to have become predictable and lacklustre, staff morale was low and the magazine was regularly upstaged by the livelier *New Statesman*'. Too often the magazine, perceived as 'a poodle for the Tory party', did not attract much interest at the newsstands.[1]

Boris, outspoken, controversial and frequently on television, seemed just the person to create a higher profile for the magazine. 'Boris has promised that he will go after scoops, but added an ominously Woosterish qualifier about scoops of ice-cream. We should not be fooled. Amid the ginger beer bonhomie resides an ambition that makes Tina Brown look like a Stepford wife.' Specifically, Johnson was seen to be the heir apparent for the top post at *The Daily Telegraph*, which, like *The Spectator*, was owned by Conrad Black. 'The battle of *The Torygraph* succession has long been won on the playing fields of *The Spectator*.'[2]

It was presumably Black's desire to keep Johnson in his employ in the long term, and at the same time to foster a degree of editorial independence from the Conservative Party, that led him to offer the post at *The Spectator* only on the condition that Boris abandon his parliamentary aspirations. Johnson, having already sought unsuccessfully a seat in both the European Parliament and Westminster, agreed. Soon thereafter, Boris resumed his search for a parliamentary seat.[3]

Johnson's change of heart may be at least partly attributable to a rocky first few months at the helm of *The Spectator*. In September, David Fingleton was named the most reliable critic

---

1 *The Times*, 30 July 1999, p. 43.

2 *The Times*, 5 August 1999, p. 21.

3 Purnell, p. 189.

in a survey of more than 4,000 restaurant-goers. Unfortunately, this came shortly after *The Spectator* fired Fingleton, who had written a column there for three years.[4]

A while later Johnson 'hotly denied' that he had failed to make his mark in the first 3 months of his editorship at around the same time that the *New Statesman*, a rival publication, announced its first profit in many years.[5] Not long thereafter, Johnson did make news, by sacking 'Britain's most unlikely rugby union correspondent, the septuagenarian Dowager Baroness Hesketh', who had covered the sport for *The Spectator* for five years.[6]

---

4 *The Times*, 24 September 1999, p. 44.
5 *The Times*, 22 October 1999, p. 48.
6 *The Times*, 17 December 1999, p. 5.

16. BORIS IS A BIFFER

That, at least, was the wry assessment of *Times* columnist Giles Coren, a connoisseur of antics Johnsonian and a prognosticator of startling acuity.

In early November 2000, Coren recounted the sad tale of Edward Leigh. The Tory MP recently had been touring his Gainsborough constituency to discuss rural crime. After a long day, he returned to the railing to which he had locked his 15-year-old bicycle, only to find that his transport had been stolen. Coren asserted that such 'joy awaits Boris', when Johnson, at the time the Tory candidate for a very safe seat, became an MP.[1]

The prescience of these words was revealed less than 3 months later, as Johnson dropped off his young son at school in Islington. Leaning his bike against a wall, he turned to kiss the boy goodbye. As he did so, a passing youth jumped on the bike. The MP-elect shouted 'Oi, you, get off my f****** bike,' and set out in pursuit. 'Imagine the terror of the scoundrel, turning to see the giant platinum-haired polemicist bearing down on him.' The thief, though pedalling furiously, was not moving very fast. So when our hero, dubbed 'Superboris' by Coren, drew near, the young man thought it expedient to abandon the bike at a zebra crossing and flee on foot. Johnson briefly gave chase but then, in his words, 'ran back to the bike to stop anyone else from nicking it'. He subsequently credited his son, who had been playing with the bike's gears on the way to school, with helping thwart the crime. However, he also could not resist the opportunity to begin acting like an Opposition MP by concluding, 'It all goes to show how [Prime Minister Tony] Blair has failed to deliver on law and order.'

Yet Johnson's attitude toward bicycle security was remarkably lackadaisical. According to a colleague at *The Spectator*, where Johnson was the editor, Boris 'never locks the bike because he

---

1 *The Times*, 2 November 2000, p. 22.

knows he'd lose the key... He just rests the lock on the bike so that it looks secure.' Johnson acknowledged that this was not his first experience with bike theft; 'I had one nicked a month ago in the same way.'[2] Does this explain the origin of Boris Bikes?

A little more than a year on, it was reported that Johnson had lost 4 bikes in his first two years in London. And even when his bike somehow miraculously escaped expropriation some considered that to be almost an injustice. When, for example, Johnson went to the British Museum with his researcher, Matthew Pencharz, in early 2002, both men chained their bikes to the same railing. When they returned, Boris's bike was still there, but Pencharz's had been stolen, something the latter found 'really quite infuriating,' particularly after the MP 'cycled off to PMQs' leaving his researcher behind to walk back to the office.[3]

2 *The Times*, 26 January 2001, p. 24.
3 *The Times*, 3 May 2002, p. 22.

17. BORIS DID NOT SACK TAKI, REPEATEDLY

Johnson took over as editor of *The Spectator* amid 'a chorus of demands' that he sack Taki Theodoracopulos, a former Greek playboy who had been writing the magazine's 'High Life' column for 22 years (except for a few months spent in prison for cocaine possession). Even in *The Spectator*, a bastion of 'right-wing fogeydom,' the columnist's published opinions were so extreme and, well, tacky, as to provoke objections. So much so that his removal was seen as something of a litmus test for the new editor: according to Ian Hislop, editor of *Private Eye*, 'If Boris sacks Taki, then I'll know he's worthy of the job.' Not long thereafter, Taki's column appeared as usual, with its author triumphantly proclaiming that he had not been sacked 'despite the pressure the scummy Left has put on the sainted editor.' Johnson confessed he had not attempted to dismiss Taki, 'as some people advised me to do'.[1]

Two years later, Conrad Black, owner of *The Spectator*, took the unusual step of using the pages of his magazine to accuse one of his employees of anti-Semitism. Taki's column had criticised Israel and depicted the American Government as suborned by Jews to do its bidding. In response, Black wrote 'In both its venomous character and its unfathomable absurdity, the farrago of lies is almost worthy of Goebbels, of the authors of the "Protocols of the Elders of Zion".' To be fair, the unfortunate columnist might have felt a little blindsided by this attack. After all, in 1997 Black had defended 'my friend Taki', after the latter wrote that Puerto Ricans in New York were 'fat, squat, ugly, dusky, dirty and unbelievably loud. They turned Manhattan into Palermo faster than you can say spic.' Still, Taki expressed contrition. Black then welcomed his 'renunciation' of anti-Semitism. And Johnson indicated that the matter was closed, and he had no intention of firing Taki.[2]

1 *The Times*, 13 August 1999, p. 3.
2 *The Times*, 3 March 2001, p. 7.

Two years on, 'Taki argued that he preferred living in Switzerland because it was free from large numbers of black people.' Blaming Home Secretary David Blunkett for a soft approach to sentencing, *The Spectator*'s columnist continued, 'Britain is being mugged by black hoodlums, people are being cut down in the streets à la Mogadishu.' Johnson admitted he was mortified by the column, which was 'a terrible thing. Very embarrassing'. But he disclaimed any responsibility, having been on holiday at the time. And his deputy had been so snowed under that he had not had time to read the column. 'But what can you do? Taki has been there for 25 years,' Johnson concluded, as if he had no say in whether the columnist made it to his 26th anniversary at the magazine.[3] The police took a rather less lenient view, investigating Johnson on a charge of incitement of racial hatred before deciding to take no further action.[4]

A few months later, Johnson suffered further humiliation when *The Spectator* published a letter from Black castigating Taki for an 'absurdly offensive' article on Richard Perle, who recently had resigned as leader of the Pentagon's Defense Policy Board. The media mogul berated his columnist for 'straying into areas that require more intellectual rigour than the mélange of pacifism and Third Reich faddism that seems to work while hobnobbing with Eurotrash and exchanging blowhardisms with Pat Buchanan'.[5]

Despite this and other criticism of Taki, including from Charles Wheeler, Johnson's father-in-law, Boris never sacked his controversial columnist.[6]

---

3 *The Times*, 16 January 2003, p. 6.
4 *The Times*, 29 September 2003, p. 4.
5 *The Times*, 16 April 2003, p. 6.
6 Purnell, p. 193.

18. BORIS WAS BEGUILED BY BUXOM BUNNIES

Like many conclaves of this nature, the 2000 Conservative Party Conference, held in Bournemouth, threatened to be a rather dull affair. Enter Giles Coren, food critic and columnist for *The Times*. After the Conference banned activists from the Anti-Vivisection Society from attending, Coren invited them to be his guests in Bournemouth, where they 'monstered' Boris Johnson.[1]

Lacking accreditation and dressed somewhat conspicuously, for a Tory Conference at least, in PVC shorts with bunny tails, tight T-shirts emblazoned with 'freedom of information', and large rabbit ears, the five 'frisky' young female activists had little chance of slipping into any of the mainstream Conference events. So they had to content themselves with attending the party's fringe meetings. Boris Johnson might have been disappointed to learn that he was not the activists' target of choice. Rather, they were 'very keen to get their teeth into John Gummer, the former Agriculture Minister, feeder of sheep to cows, and cows to daughters'. However, possibly forewarned, 'he's hopped it.' But their entrance did not go unnoticed, for the bunnies were forced to endure 'the wolf-whistles of Tory delegates who clearly had not seen a woman under 90 in months'.[2]

Speaking at the gathering when the bunnies arrived was Boris Johnson, who, though not yet himself an MP, already was seeking to impart a little star power to the party. 'Mr Johnson looked momentarily flustered by the bobtails and T-shirts, but then being momentarily flustered is Mr Johnson's stock-in-trade.' Things quickly went from bad to worse. Speakers were asked to name a brave, unpopular action that Conservative Party Leader William Hague should take. 'Wear a dress?' Johnson spluttered, momentarily flustered. Then he had a better idea: 'Call for the reintroduction of crucifixion?' The idea was

---

1 *The Times*, 29 December 2000, p. 24.
2 *The Times*, 3 October 2000, p. 18.

met by a low rumble of support from root-and-branch Tory activists. Boris then 'protested that if the challenge was to think of ways to make William Hague more unpopular, then "my imagination just isn't up to it."' As it became clear that this comment 'might be horribly misinterpreted, Johnson became momentarily flustered and retreated into a prolonged splutter.'[3]

Just when it seemed that he had lost the plot, Johnson managed to save the day. He pointed out that he once had worked for the International Fund for Animal Welfare. Lending his support to the activists and their cause therefore was not out of the question. As bunnies 'swarmed all over him demanding photos, he remembered what he was going into politics for.'[4]

3 *The Times*, 3 October 2000, p. 10.
4 *The Times*, 3 October 2000, p. 18.

19. BORIS WAS ELECTED MP FOR HENLEY IN 2001

Less than two years after unsuccessfully standing for Clwyd South, a safe Labour seat, Johnson was said to be 'barking after the Tory nomination in Sutton and Cheam', a constituency the Conservatives had held for decades prior to the 1997 Labour landslide.[1] However, a few months later he was appointed editor of *The Spectator*, reportedly only on the condition that he abandon his political ambitions. Yet soon thereafter it became clear that Johnson still was on the lookout for a parliamentary seat.[2]

He soon set his eyes on Henley, one of the safest Tory seats in the country, having returned Michael Heseltine with a majority of over 11,000 in the 1997 general election. The veteran MP's decision to retire prompted dozens of aspirants to apply to the Henley Conservative Association to become its nominee. Despite a similar untamed coiffure, Johnson was quite different from the man whose shoes he hoped to fill. Heseltine was a supporter of the Euro who had been instrumental in the replacement of one Tory leader (Margaret Thatcher) and conspicuously critical of another (William Hague). Johnson, by contrast, was a 'Thatcherite stormtrooper' who, like Hague, strongly supported Britain retaining the pound as its currency. Indeed, the two men were such opposites politically that some who disliked the incumbent MP seemed willing to support Boris out of spite. 'It would be worth it,' said a former association officer, 'just to see Heseltine choke.'[3]

By July 2000, the field had been winnowed to three potential nominees: Boris Johnson, London barrister David Platt and Jill Andrew, who had stood in Walthamstow in the previous election. Ominously for his rivals, the winner was to be chosen under a new format curiously similar to

1 *The Times*, 8 March 1999, p. 20.

2 *The Times*, 18 September 1999, p. 20.

3 *The Times*, 9 June 2000, p. 15.

the BBC's satirical show, *Have I Got News for You*, on which Johnson famously had appeared. Instead of each finalist facing queries from association members individually, as had been the procedure previously, all three would now appear together to face 'quick-fire questions' from both members and each other. It was to be 'a battle to establish the quickest, wittiest, most accomplished performer and to uncover the one who wilts under pressure'.[4] No points for guessing who came out on top!

In the 2001 General Election, Johnson beat his nearest competitor, Liberal Democrat Catherine Bearder, by more than 8,000 votes. His triumph amid another Labour landslide set some hearts aflutter. One woman wrote to *The Times* that while her husband and many of his friends saw Johnson as a future Prime Minister, she feared he was overqualified for the post: 'He is too witty, articulate and delightfully irreverent for this to be even a distant dream.' However, another correspondent was decidedly less enthusiastic, arguing that Henley was such a dyed-in-the wool Tory constituency that its voters 'would, given half a chance, elect a pink blancmange if it had a blue ribbon round it. On reflection, that is exactly what they did.'[5]

Perhaps the only blemish on the day was a picture, widely disseminated, of the victorious candidate sitting next to his wife, mouth agape. He later conceded, typically, 'I yawn prodigiously, a real exhibition of the epiglottis.'[6] For critics, however, it was not the reflex action but the failure to cover his mouth with his hand that was the real *faux pas*: 'Surely a true peroxide-blue Tory, representative of the ruling classes and, nay, even editor of *The Spectator*, ought to know better?'[7]

---

4 *The Times*, 12 July 2000, p. 6.
5 *The Times*, 8 October 2001, p. 21.
6 *The Times*, 1 October 2001, p. 4 (S).
7 *The Times*, 13 October 2001, p. 17 (S).

20. BORIS WROTE A BOOK ABOUT BECOMING MP FOR HENLEY IN 2001

Typically, Johnson turned his experiences on the campaign trail into a book. *Friends, Voters, Countrymen: Jottings on the Stump*, was entertaining more than insightful. Indeed, a review in *The Guardian* interpreted it as 'yet another sign of Tory decline' that the party's most promising new MP opted to publish his political memoirs only weeks after entering Westminster.[1] Still, the book is not without interest, particularly in light of subsequent events.

Johnson wrote, 'What I hated about Brussels was not just our national impotence, but the lying, our lying.' (As someone with some experience and expertise in dissimulation, it is not clear whether Boris is envious of the powers of prevarication of some of his countrymen or contemptuously regards them as mere amateurs, compared to himself.) British ministers, Boris continued, talked about standing up to Europe only to 'cheerfully surrender' something that they now said was not actually all that important in the interests of getting some other bureaucratic concession. 'Matters of national policy, agreed on in Cabinet and bearing the stamp of British democratic approval, were just a bit of negotiating capital.' In his telling, such views put Johnson in a tight spot. To 'proper' Europhiles, like Michael Heseltine, the man he was seeking to replace as MP for Henley, Boris 'was a monster who wanted to cut Britain adrift'. Still, Johnson characterises as 'total balls' rumours that he struck a deal with Heseltine whereby the latter would instruct his pro-Europe followers to support Johnson in return for the latter backing Ken Clarke for the Tory leadership. On the other hand, 'proper' Eurosceptics disdained to support Johnson in favour of the UK Independence Party, with one going so far as to slap one of the Tory candidate's campaign stickers on the seat of his trousers contemptuously while telling him, 'It'll blow off when I fart.'[2]

1 'Sign of the Times,' by Will Buckley, 21 October 2001, theguardian.com
2 *The Times*, 27 September 2001, p. 20.

At one point, Johnson was joined on the campaign trail by 'the nation's premier broadcaster', Jeremy Paxman, who asked the candidate why he wanted to become an MP when journalists were far more influential. Johnson replied, 'it's 30 per cent a desire to be of public service or use ... it's 40 per cent sheer egomania; and it is 30 per cent attributable to the belief that the world ought not to be run by swankpot journalists, showing off and kicking politicians around, when they haven't tried to do any better themselves.'[3]

Although Johnson professed support for 'controlled immigration', something 'the country needs', he dismissed much of the debate on the topic as 'bogus'. 'While there may have been "waves" of immigration previously, the nation's bloodstock has been stable and homogenous for the past 1,000 years.' This makes the level of post-war immigration, which 'is about to produce Asian majorities in Leeds and Bradford', a new phenomenon. This is not necessarily bad. Johnson's optimistic view is that this could produce 'a new syncretic British culture, absorbing the best from each immigrant population'. This would be 'better than a 'multicultural society of mutually segregated ethnic groups, each with a vast apparatus of lawyers and lobbyists, and an eternal feeling of grievance'.[4]

Johnson claimed to have been worried that defeat would cause him to 'flee blubbing to New South Wales to take up a career selling Nature's Raw Guarana to the housewives of Wollongong', but fate had other plans for him.[5]

---

3 *The Times*, 28 September 2001, p. 2 (S1).
4 *The Times*, 29 September 2001, p. 17.
5 *The Times*, 1 October 2001, p. 4 (S).

21. BORIS IS A 'CRINGING SYCOPHANT'

In the 2001 General Election, Labour retained the huge parliamentary majority it had won in 1997 while the Conservatives managed to gain only 1 additional seat. In response to this dismal showing, Tory leader William Hague resigned. The contest to succeed him featured 5 candidates: Michael Ancram, David Davis, Kenneth Clarke, Iain Duncan Smith, and Michael Portillo.

The procedure was for the party's MPs to whittle down the candidates to a pair, with the party's full membership then choosing between them. More than a week before the first round, Boris Johnson was listed as a probable supporter of Clarke's candidacy, rather than that of Portillo, the presumed frontrunner.[1] In the first ballot, on 10 July, Johnson indicated that he has supported Clarke.[2] He supported him again in the second ballot 2 days later.[3] In the third ballot, Clarke won the most votes, with Duncan Smith second, meaning the party's membership would choose its new leader from between the two.

In the ensuing campaign, Johnson was one of 26 MPs and peers who publicly backed Clarke, less for his (moderate) views on Europe than because they thought he could win an election. To counter the impression that he was soft on Europe, Clarke sought to portray Duncan Smith as a hard-line Eurosceptic who wanted to take Britain out of the European Union. This prompted Duncan Smith's spokesman to state that his boss 'had never contemplated Britain withdrawing from the EU. It is complete rubbish.'[4] Tory voters backed Duncan Smith by a wide margin.

So, it was a little awkward when, writing in *Conservative Heartland* about 2 months later, Johnson extolled the new Tory leader as having 'rock-solid right-wing credentials' and knowing 'exactly how he is going to take on Labour'.

1 *The Times*, 29 June 2001, p. 12.
2 *The Times*, 11 July 2001, p. 4.
3 *The Times*, 13 July 2001, p. 4
4 *The Times*, 20 August 2001, p. 8.

Johnson pointed out that that he had identified Duncan Smith as a worthy Tory leader in an article he had written for *The Daily Telegraph* in 1994, neatly eliding his support for a different candidate for the job only weeks earlier. 'Call me a cringing sycophant,' the MP for Henley gushed, 'but I very much like Iain Duncan Smith.'[5]

Less than two years later, Johnson's views had changed for he was one of the Tory MPs who supported a vote of no confidence in the party leader. Its passage led to his resignation. But even after wielding the knife, Johnson exhibited traces of his former obsequiousness, lamenting 'Even among the 90 of us who voted to end Iain Duncan Smith's leadership, there was real sadness at his passing.' [6] Cold comfort, no doubt.

5 *The Times*, 17 November 2001, p. 24.
6 *The Times*, 31 October 2003, p. 2 (S).

22. BORIS WAS INVOLVED IN A ROW OVER THE QUEEN MOTHER'S FUNERAL

When Queen Elizabeth, the Queen Mother, died at age 101 in late March 2002, plans were of course already in place to provide an appropriate ceremonial send off. She would lie in state for three days in Westminster Hall, where an estimated 200,000 people would pay their respects. Later, more than a million people would gather outside Westminster Abbey for the funeral services, and line the streets leading from there to Windsor Castle, her final resting place.

All that attention was hard for a politician to resist, at least according to some reports. Writing in *The Spectator*, Peter Osborne, the magazine's political editor, claimed that Prime Minister Tony Blair, acting through his private secretary, had sought to alter the arrangements for when the Queen Mother's coffin arrived in Westminster Hall to give himself greater prominence. Although both 10 Downing Street and the office of Black Rod, the parliamentary organiser of the event, issued denials, two other newspapers subsequently repeated (and expanded upon) the claims. A spokesman for the Prime Minister responded by stating that the notion that his boss 'would seek to exploit the death of the Queen Mother is totally without foundation and deeply offensive'. The administration filed a formal complaint with the Press Complaints Commission, an action Blair had taken before, but typically only in response to coverage of his children. *The Spectator*'s editor, Boris Johnson, replied, 'We are confident in our story and will be fighting this all the way.'[1]

Less than 2 months later, Downing Street dropped the complaint. Alastair Campbell, Blair's director of communication, indicated there was no need to pursue the matter because no evidence had been presented that the Prime Minister had been personally involved. While Campbell conceded that Blair's aide had been in touch with Black Rod, that had been merely

---

1 *The Times*, 24 April 2002, p. 2.

to find out what was expected of the Prime Minister at the ceremony. However, Johnson characterised the withdrawal of the complaint as a 'ludicrous and humiliating' climbdown, asserting that his publication had never claimed the Prime Minister phoned Black Rod personally, only that calls had been made on the former's behalf. 'The more the story was investigated the clearer it was that Tony Blair tried to aggrandise his role in the Queen Mother's lying in state,' concluded *The Spectator's* editor.[2]

A few days later, in what might have been seen as a case of the pot calling the kettle black, Johnson averred, 'It has long been known that Tony Blair is not shy of publicity. Give him a spotlight and he will somehow use his elbows so as to place himself beneath it.'[3]

2 *The Times*, 12 June 2002, p. 10.
3 *The Times*, 15 June 2002, p. 12.

23. BORIS'S *SPECTATOR* NAMED TONY BLAIR 2002 PARLIAMENTARIAN OF THE YEAR

In November 2002 the 19th annual Parliamentarian of the Year awards were presented in London. Boris Johnson, editor of *The Spectator*, one of the awards' sponsors, served as chairman of the judges. Prime Minister Tony Blair was accorded the honour. Explaining the judges' reasoning, Johnson said that Blair 'can do cool; he can do Churchill; he can do cool Churchill: "You know, guys, it's blood, toil, tears and sweat."' Boris cautioned that, 'this award is primarily a recognition of the parliamentary achievement of a man whose government is not universally thought to have been good for parliamentary democracy.' In other words, it resulted from Blair's utter dominance of the parliamentary scene. Judges were said to have remarked of Blair's performance: 'He's on top of his game'; 'He's on mid-season form'; or simply that he was 'the coolest cat in town'.[1]

Given that *The Spectator* was aligned with the Conservative Party, and Blair 'is regularly criticised for being the man who has done more than any other to side-line the House of Commons and Parliament', many MPs were surprised by the decision, according to the BBC. 'The first reaction by many was that the magazine editor and Tory MP, the mop-haired funster Boris Johnson, was taking the mickey with the award.'[2]

Yet even before the award was announced, Johnson sought to distance himself from it. As Ben Macintyre, one of the judges, opined, 'If deniability is a key to political success then Boris is going places.' Although the judges collectively decided that Blair deserved the honour, Johnson 'managed to make it sound as if he'd just wandered in from the street to find, golly, that the Prime Minister had been chosen. This is the unique Johnsonian knack.' He similarly had sought

---

1 'Parliamentarian of the Year,' 23 November 2002, spectator.co.uk.
2 '*Spectator* Picks Blair for top award,' by Nick Assinder, 21 November 2002, news.bbc.co.uk.

to appear to sort of stumble into Henley's parliamentary seat and *The Spectator*'s editorship. Ironically, this made him the antithesis of his laureate. 'Mr Johnson is a master at pretending to be slightly at sea when anything but; in that he is the quintessential un-Blair, who cannot bear anyone to suspect that he is not in total control, all the time.'[3]

Johnson's distancing act did not appear to be all that effective for, a few days later, it was reported that he was 'reacting badly to the deluge of criticism over his craven decision' to give the award to Blair. During a somewhat rare appearance in the Commons, Boris 'flashed a V-sign at Quentin Letts, a sketch writer, who had led the critical charge'. This unparliamentary gesture was not detected by the Speaker. So, undeterred, Johnson also gave 'a variation on the Churchillian salute' to Frank Johnson, a former editor of *The Spectator*.[4]

3 *The Times*, 22 November 2002, p. 2.
4 *The Times*, 27 November 2002, p. 6.

24. BORIS WAS BATTERED BY BUNS BUT THE EGGS MISSED

The first decade of the twenty-first century was an interesting time to be a politician in Britain. Attacking MPs with comestibles became something of a fad. Prime Minister Tony Blair was hit with a tomato. Three women wielding custard pies attacked International Development Secretary Clare Short. Agriculture Minister Nick Brown had a chocolate éclair shoved into his face. It got so bad that bookmakers were accepting bets on which pudding would next be used against which minister.[1]

Boris Johnson, so often *sui generis*, on this occasion was merely part of a trend. In early 2002 the MP addressed the Mayor of Henley's annual dinner. In the course of his remarks he indicated that he often was asked what policies the Conservatives had to offer. He continued, 'At the risk of being hit by a bread roll I shall tell you some of my ideas.' He went on to expound upon the lamentable state of public services, Henley's roads, and rising crime. When he began to discuss nurses' pay, he was struck in the face by a 'mini French baguette'. Tony Lane, Mayor of Henley, claimed never to have seen anything as disgraceful in his 37 years in local government. Johnson's assailant, Eleanor Hards, the (Labour) chairwoman of the South Oxfordshire District Council, who had been sitting three seats away from the MP at the top table, was unapologetic. 'He deserved it. He was making an overtly party-political speech, worthy of the Tory conference. He mentioned at least three times that people threw bread rolls at him when they got bored. So I took him at his word.'[2]

Four years later a reader e-mailed Hugo Rifkind, a columnist at *The Times*, to recount an interesting incident he had recently witnessed. The reader had been in a shop on Highbury

---

1 Wolfe, Eugene L., *Dangerous Seats: Parliamentary Violence in the United Kingdom*, (Stroud, Gloucestershire: Amberley, 2019), pp. 283–5.
2 Gimson, p. 146.

Corner when in rushed an 'odd-looking fellow' who asked for some eggs, telling the owner he would return in 5 minutes to pay for them. Intrigued, the witness followed the man out of the store, where he observed Boris Johnson crossing the street. The fellow with the eggs began throwing them at the MP. 'Boris started effing and blinding and tried to push the man away in a rather girly way with his knees.' A cab arrived. 'Boris got in, but then decided to get out again, to hurl some abuse. In all the excitement, he fell over.'[3]

Rifkind's column prompted an early morning call from Johnson, who told him the 'important point' in the story was that 'the tosser missed. I am a corpulent Conservative shadow minister. Not a small target. Yet not one drop of albumen spattered my suit. A terrible indictment of the sporting ability of today's youth. I blame the Government. No wonder we lost so badly to Bangladesh. Or whoever.'[4]

3 *The Times*, 27 June 2006, p. 12.
4 *The Times*, 28 June 2006, p. 4.

25. BORIS CARES ABOUT BIRDS (AND GOATS AND PIGS)

One of the main constitutional functions of Members of Parliament is to hold the government accountable. One way to do this is to pose questions to ministers. The topics covered can vary considerably. If, in his early years as an MP, Boris Johnson did not exactly become a champion for all creatures great and small, he did demonstrate concern for the welfare of a few specific members of the animal kingdom.

In 1998 Customs seized three Lear's macaws that had been smuggled into Britain by Henry Sissen. He ended up serving 18 months in prison, but the birds' confinement was considerably longer. Three years after their seizure, they remained trapped by legal procedures in a Yorkshire bird sanctuary. This was a problem not only for the macaws in question but also for their entire species, only 246 are left in the wild. Environmentalists were hoping to return the seized birds to their native Brazil for breeding.[1]

Enter Boris Johnson. In mid-October 2001 the MP for Henley posed a written question to the Chancellor of the Exchequer seeking information both on the Customs and Excise investigation of the case and the prospects of returning the macaws to Brazil. The Government responded that Sissen had appealed both a £150,000 confiscation order (representing the amount he was thought to have received for smuggling the birds into the country) and the seizure of the macaws. Customs was unable to decide the fate of the birds until the legal proceedings were completed.[2]

A few months later, Johnson was at it again, scrutinising the Government's policy toward goats. Specifically, he asked if goats were to be tested with sheep for BSE (mad cow disease) and, should sheep test positive for the disease, whether the 'national goat herd' would have to be destroyed.

1 *The Times*, 10 December 2001, p. 9.
2 'Lear's Macaws,' 15 October 2001, vol. 372, hansard.parliament.uk.

The Government confirmed that goats would be tested with sheep, but noted that the consequences for the former should the latter test positive would depend on both the 'circumstances at the time' and advice from relevant authorities. Johnson followed up by inquiring about the reasons for recent regulatory changes regarding the transport of goats for mating. The Government responded that movement of animals had been restricted to limit the spread of foot-and-mouth disease.[3]

And two years after that, it was pigs, or at least those who cared for them, that were the subject of a Johnsonian intervention. In early 2004 he claimed that the Government had a moral duty to provide compensation to the 62 pig swill providers who had been banned from distributing their product during the 2001 foot-and-mouth outbreak. The ban not only hurt distributors but also resulted in an additional 1.7 million tonnes of banana skins, potato shavings and other waste, much of which went down the drain, resulting in clogged sewers and vermin infestations. Summing up his case for the swill-feeders in typical style, Johnson concluded, 'They may be involved in a mucky business but that is no reason to treat them like muck.'[4]

In late 2006 residents of Beckenham, in south-east London, received a notice through their letterboxes reading 'Lost: Large pure white male cat. New to the area. Loves to remove his collar. Friendly. Answers to the name of "Boris Johnson". Neutered.'[5]

Perhaps not coincidentally shortly thereafter Johnson told a packed meeting in his constituency that he was determined to track down their pets, 53 of which had been reported stolen in the previous half-year.[6]

3 Hansard HC Deb 22 January 2002 vol 378 cc783–4W.
4 *The Times*, 17 March 2004, p. 2.
5 *The Times*, 10 November 2006, p. 15.
6 *The Times*, 12 March 2007, p. 13.

26. BORIS LONG HAS PLAYED THE 'ANTI-POLITICIAN'

Part of Boris's tremendous appeal is that he does not look like a typical politician. The stereotypical MP goes about looking as if ready for a potential encounter with a television camera, with hair perfectly coiffed and clothes carefully selected to present the desired professional image. Boris does things differently. He sports a hairstyle fellow journalist-turned-politician Michael Gove once described as 'like a Tongan's skirt'.[1] Gove later added that Johnson 'looks as though he got dressed in the rear gunner's turret of a Lancaster bomber during a particularly difficult night over Hamburg'.[2] His disdain for an iron and a comb are legendary. According to Matthew Parris, the politician-turned-journalist, 'Nobody has ever seen Mr Johnson kempt and the suspicion grows that he sleeps standing on his head and re-rumples his hair regularly throughout the day.'[3]

Johnson's professed views often are far from politically correct. Where many leading politicians were at pains to disclaim or minimise their youthful chemical indiscretions, Boris feigned offence that he might be thought similarly abstemious, stating in response to intimations that he might not have indulged, 'This is an outrageous slur. Of course I've taken drugs.'[4] Similarly, when asked for his views on allowing pubs to stay open so customers could drink 24-hours a day, he told the Oxford Union that he was 'very attracted' to the idea, adding, 'I may be diverting from Tory party policy here, but I don't care.'[5] And, lamenting on the pages of *The Spectator* the costs to local councils of cleaning gum off pavements, he asks a heretical rhetorical question, 'Wouldn't it be cheaper if we all just took

1 *The Times*, 1 September 2001, p. 12.
2 *The Times*, 9 May 2007, p. 7 (S).
3 *The Times*, 3 October 2001, p. 10.
4 *The Times*, 22 October 2005, p. 3.
5 *The Times*, 30 April 2005, p. 42.

up smoking?'[6] He earlier had opposed a ban on smoking in pubs and restaurants, indicating the dangers were exaggerated.[7]

A typical politician, when asked about the party's dismal prospects in an upcoming election, would respond with anodyne denials or political bromides. Not Boris. When queried about the travails of the Conservative Party several months before he supported a vote of no confidence in leader Ian Duncan Smith, Johnson, a classicist at Oxford, not only embraced the notion that the Tories were in trouble but described its tribulations in a way that was inimitably his own: 'One thinks of Erisichthon, the person who ended up self-cannibalistically gnawing his entrails; or of Narcissus, also commemorated by Ovid, who spent so long gazing at his own reflection in a pool that he went into a trance, toppled in and drowned. The behaviour of Onan does not seem entirely irrelevant.'[8]

Refreshing and endearing though such behaviour may seem, it is, like the actions of more conventional politicians, at least something of an act. Johnson cultivates the persona of an amiable bumbler along the lines of the fictional Bertie Wooster, with whom he is often compared. Indeed, Johnson was elected patron of the P. G. Wodehouse Society, presumably largely due to his resemblance to the author's most famous and beloved character and his penchant for Wodehousian expressions such as 'spiffing'.[9] But not everybody was taken in. Johnson's appearance, demeanour and views all seemed at least somewhat calculated to set him apart, to appeal to a constituency that disdains traditional politicians. Seeming different, unconventional, iconoclastic even, was to be Boris's ultimate path to power, and he knew it. As Ben Macintyre argued, 'Nobody plays the anti-politician better than Boris Johnson, while remaining political to the core.'[10]

---

6 *The Times*, 12 April 2005, p. 2 (S1).
7 *The Times*, 25 September 2004, p. 29.
8 *The Times*, 4 March 2003, p. 4 (S).
9 *The Times*, 4 December 2002, p. 6.
10 *The Times*, 19 April 2005, p. 18.

27. BORIS BIKES

Long before he became identified with facilitating the rental of the eponymous means of transportation, Boris was on his bike. The MP for Henley regularly commuted between his home in Islington and Westminster on two wheels. In the process Johnson, who only began riding seriously in 1999, soon became 'perhaps the most famous cyclist in Britain'.[1] His fame spread not only because of his method of locomotion, or because the sight of the hulking, dishevelled parliamentarian perched somewhat precariously on a bike was, well, something of a sight, but also because Boris's adventures and misadventures on two wheels were legion and legendary.

One problem is that Boris rarely does just one thing at a time, and it can be dangerous to combine cycling with other activities. A few months after the incident at the British Museum a fellow cyclist was alarmed to see Johnson 'wobbling along on his bike while simultaneously conducting a conversation on his mobile phone'. When she attempted to remonstrate with him, 'he reportedly responded with the most unparliamentary retort of "bollocks".'[2] He followed up in print by calling her 'the kind of bossy Islingtonian female who becomes health minister in the new Labour Government.' She responded, in a letter to the newspaper, by saying she was a Tory voter.[3] However, six weeks later, having reportedly taken to heart criticism that he was endangering himself and other while conducting both parliamentary and journalistic business while astride his bike, Johnson was said to be 'thinking of getting a bracket for his mobile fitted to his handlebars'.[4]

Typically, Johnson's close encounters of the two-wheeled kind provided penetrating insight into fundamental social divisions. He observed, 'Cyclists see motorists as tyrannical and uncaring. Motorists believe cyclists are afflicted by a perversion.

---

1 Gimson, p. 182.
2 *The Times*, 6 August 2002, p. 7 (S).
3 *The Times*, 6 December 2004, p. 5.
4 *The Times*, 27 September 2002, p. 19 (S).

It is like the tension between gays and straights in the Fifties.'[5] A year later, he suggested that reconciliation was his priority: 'There is no love lost between cyclists and motorists ... my political mission is to heal the rift. As between the Hutus and the Tutsis, we must have a grand rapprochement.'[6]

Perhaps this objective helps explain why Johnson's support of cycling was at least somewhat ambivalent. When, in early 2004, the Government announced plans to almost triple the mileage allowance (from 7.2p to 20p per mile) for MPs who cycled to work, Johnson indicated he was opposed to the move: 'I am all for encouraging cycling, but not at taxpayers' expense.'[7]

However, several months later, after his Tories sought to amend a Road Safety Bill to make cyclists liable for the same fines as drivers for using mobiles, Johnson pledged 'to defend the right to cycle and phone while there is breath in my body'. He added, 'Just as I will never vote to ban hunting, so I will never vote to abolish the free-born Englishman's time-hallowed and immemorial custom, dating back as far as 1990 or so, of cycling while talking on a mobile.' He later told *London Cyclist* magazine that, even after the encounter with the woman from Islington, he still used his mobile while cycling. 'It's not against the law. If I was a one-armed cyclist you wouldn't kick me off my bicycle, and I'm just doing something with my free arm, aren't I?'[8]

---

5 *The Times*, 31 May 2003, p. 18 (S).
6 *The Times*, 3 December 2004, p. 2 (S).
7 *The Times*, 27 January 2004, p. 10.
8 *The Times*, 6 December 2004, p. 5.

28. BORIS WAS MOCKED AS AN 'OCCASIONAL' MP

When Johnson became MP for Henley in 2001, he was already stretched quite thin. He was editor of *The Spectator*, had a column in *The Telegraph* and *GQ*, made frequent appearances on television, and wrote a book or two in his copious spare time. This was alarming to some of his employers. Indeed, to get to this point, he had to deceive two of them. To become editor, he had promised Conrad Black, the *Spectator*'s owner, that he would not run for Parliament. And to become MP, he had promised Henley that he would resign as editor. He later tried to placate his constituents by claiming, apparently untruthfully, that he had relinquished some of his *Spectator* salary because he editorial role there had been reduced. In the end, however, Johnson betrayed both Black and Henley.[1]

So, it is perhaps not surprising that Johnson's early parliamentary career was less than splendid. Assigned to a committee charged with the time-consuming task of reviewing a major piece of legislation, Boris sometimes arrived late, if he turned up at all. This was to be something of a pattern. He ranked 525th out of 659 MPs for attendance, having managed to take part in just over half the Commons' votes in his first four years. In his second Parliament, his attendance fell to 45 per cent, to the consternation of his colleagues and party whips. And when he did turn up, he failed to impress. Indeed, he later described his own parliamentary performance as 'crap'.[2]

It presumably was due not just to professional jealousy that Johnson regularly was referred to in the press as the 'occasional' MP for Henley. In fact, there were repeated questions about how seriously he was taking his parliamentary duties. One journalist, passing by the MP's open office door, reportedly heard his secretary respond to a telephone inquiry thus: 'Oh no, Boris isn't here today... He's over at his proper job at *The Spectator*.'[3]

1 Purnell, pp. 226–7.
2 Ibid., pp. 225, 232–3.
3 *The Times*, 23 January 2002, p. 16.

Another provided this tip to overstretched Johnson: 'If you ever need a resting place between media events, Boris, there's a great snooze spot in that funny Gothic building by Big Ben. It's called the Commons.'[4]

Perhaps nobody ridiculed Boris Johnson's lack of dedication to his Commons' duties more mercilessly than Frank Johnson, no relation, 'the doyen of parliamentary sketch-writers'. Boris had replaced Frank as editor of *The Spectator*, and both wrote columns for *The Daily Telegraph*, so it may have been that familiarity bred a certain contempt. In any event, Frank's criticism of Boris evidently hit home, for in early 2002 the latter wrote a letter to *The Telegraph* castigating the former for writing a sketch without visiting the Commons. Frank responded that had relied on television coverage of a sitting of Parliament while sick at home. He also claimed victory, asserting that his criticisms of Boris had forced him to attend Parliament more assiduously: 'It would probably be fair to say that far from neglecting his duties as an MP, he's in the chamber so much he's probably neglecting his duties as editor of *The Spectator*.'[5] Maybe, but little more than a week later, Boris was seen mouthing something to Frank, who reportedly had been 'campaigning selflessly' to persuade the MP 'not to wear himself out by slaving night and day in the House of Commons'. The word not voiced was, according to different observers, 'Tanker', 'Banker', or 'Wonka'.[6]

---

4 *The Times*, 26 December 2002, p. 6.
5 *The Times*, 14 February 2003, p. 6.
6 *The Times*, 25 February 2003, p. 2.

29. BORIS BECAME A SHADOW MINISTER

In an apparent effort to improve discipline, new Tory leader Michael Howard appointed more than half (88 of 165) of the party's backbenchers to front-bench positions. Boris Johnson's selection as Conservative Party vice-chairman with special responsibility for campaigning 'was one of the eye-catching appointments' made in late 2003.[1] According to a biographer, 'Boris's gift for cheering up the rank and file had been recognised. His talents were apparently so big that he could not be ignored.'[2]

In May 2004, Johnson was appointed shadow arts minister. Almost immediately, he laid out his programme, one element of which was: 'I am going to open up the bandwidth so much there is much more freedom on radio stations. I am going to reduce some of the stuff allocated to the Pentagon so you can get the Rolling Stones in Oxfordshire.'[3] Other policies included instituting 'a Windows spell-check in English so that schoolchildren in this country no longer feel they have got it wrong when they spell it correctly', and giving the Greeks 'and indistinguishable replica of all the Parthenon marbles, done in the most beautiful marble' to end that particular controversy.[4]

Things did not really improve thereafter. As the tenth anniversary of the national lottery approached, Johnson called it 'a Tory triumph,' perhaps forgetting that he previously had characterised it as 'a tax on stupidity'.[5]

In his debut appearance as shadow arts minister at Culture, Media and Sport Questions, Johnson's delivery was 'rushed, rambling and staccato'. The issue was playing fields. He asserted that while Labour had promised to ban the sale of such fields, applications to do exactly that had risen every year. In the previous year, 440 successful applications 'led to the

1 *The Times*, 12 November 2003, p. 12.
2 Gimson, pp. 179–9.
3 *The Times*, 10 May 2004, p. 2 (S).
4 Gimson, p. 179.
5 *The Times*, 14 May 2004, p. 6.

total extinction of those facilities'. Amid shouts of 'Too long!' Johnson tried to continue, 'Will the minister tell us what he has in mind urging people to run down concrete roads...' There was more shouting and burbling and finally Boris ended with something about arresting the decline in playing fields.[6]

At the Conservative Conference in Bournemouth in October 2004, Johnson was confronted with the question of how to make the Tory party cool. His response, 'I don't think we need to breakdance around Whitehall,' evoked nervous laughter. Boris reassured colleagues that 'very shortly' the party would be both chic and cool. In any event, he continued, 'What could be less cool, frankly, than voting for Tony Blair?' In response to this rhetorical question, *Times* columnist Ann Treneman answered, 'Actually there may be quite a few things. Some of them right here in Bournemouth.'[7]

Assessing Johnson's performance a few months after his appointment, Richard Morrison asserted that Michael Howard should be upset 'by the booming vacuum where his Shadow Arts Minister's arts policies ought to be'. With the Government widely detested for introducing social-engineering targets and marginalising the teaching of music, drama and art in State schools, even 'a half-awake Opposition arts spokesman' should have had an easy time effectively criticising the Blair administration's policies. 'Yet Boris has fumbled chance after chance to score points in these furious debates.' When the Government introduced a 'Music Manifesto', Johnson did not blast it for failing to provide additional funding for music teaching but instead promised that the Tories would 'bring back hymns in school assemblies'. Morrison summarised Johnson's ministerial performance as, 'fatuous, out-of-touch and intellectually lazy'.[8]

6 *The Times*, 25 May 2004, p. 2.
7 *The Times*, 7 October 2004, p. 2.
8 *The Times*, 25 October 2004, p. 2 (S).

30. BORIS WROTE A MOTORING COLUMN FOR *GQ*

In 1999 Johnson began writing articles about cars for the men's magazine *GQ*. His 'fixation for sexually charged language' came through as he reviewed the expensive, 'babe magnet' sports cars that he was given to test drive at his leisure. Read now, the *GQ* output comes across as the outpourings of a sex-obsessed cross between Jeremy Clarkson and Toad of Toad Hall. There is talk of blonde drivers 'waggling their rumps', his own superior horsepower 'taking them from behind', aided by tantalising thoughts of the imaginary 'ample bosoms' of the female SatNav voice. Driving a Ferrari F430, according to Boris, was 'as though the whole county of Hampshire was laying back and opening her well-bred legs to be ravished by the Italian stallion'. Later, even he was forced to admit that the *GQ* pieces suffered from a 'sprinkling of desperate sexual metaphors'.[1]

Sexually charged language was hardly the only problem. Johnson's *GQ* column might well have been the most expensive in the magazine's history. This was not only because Boris was paid quite well to write it but also because of his blithe indifference to normal rules of motoring. 'He collected dozens of parking tickets and fines by casually double-parking cars outside the likes of New Scotland Yard or the Royal Festival Hall. Penalty notices were, in Boris's own words, "building up like drifting snow on the windshield" and more than once an underling had to be dispatched to rescue the car from the pound.' *GQ*, not Boris, inevitably ended up footing the bill.[2]

There were other issues. Sometimes Boris could not find the car that had been delivered. It did not help that he could not even recall what colour it was. Then there was the fact that the functionality of some of these high-performance vehicles was not, shall we say, intuitive. Which made it potentially

---

1 Purnell, pp. 171–2.
2 ibid., p. 172.

problematic that, 'Boris tended to miss the session at which he would have been shown by the delivery driver how to use the car.' Sometimes he sent Mary Wakefield, a colleague at *The Spectator*, to take the lesson in his place. Once, on a Saturday, he called her to ask how to open the car's door. He apparently was stuck inside, at least until she informed him that a little dial had to be turned for egress.[3]

Finally, when he could operate them, driving flash cars to Westminster did not endear Johnson to fellow MPs, many of whom already were irked that he was not devoting more time to his parliamentary duties. 'It is also fair to say that he would on occasion rile his colleagues by flaunting whatever Maserati, Ferrari or Bentley he was test-driving that month.'[4]

3 Gimson, p. 178.
4 Purnell, p. 226.

31. BORIS WAS NOMINATED FOR A BAFTA AWARD

Although Johnson got his start as a journalist, he soon branched out into other media. In the 1980s and 1990s he was featured on radio programmes dozens of times. In early 1998 he appeared on an episode of the TV show *Have I Got News for You*. His performance, reminiscent of P. G. Wodehouse's Bertie Wooster, was such a hit that more television invitations followed, including *Question Time*, *Top Gear*, *Parkinson* and *Breakfast with Frost*.[1]

Johnson's appearances on television brought not only increasing public recognition but also a measure of critical acclaim: in 2004 he was nominated for a British Academy of Film and Television Arts award for Best Entertainment Performance on Television for his role as guest host of *Have I Got News for You*.[2] Typically, Johnson self-deprecatingly disclaimed any credit for the accolade, telling *Heat* magazine, 'I am like a fat German tourist, hoisted up to the top of Everest by a team of Sherpas, some of whom died on the way up.'[3]

Alas, he did not quite manage to reach the summit. Jonathan Ross took home the 2004 Bafta TV award, besting not only Boris but also Stephen Fry and Paul Merton.

Johnson had better luck when he stuck to writing. In 1997 he was named Commentator of the Year at the 'What the Papers Say' awards.[4] Eight years later, Johnson's writing in *The Daily Telegraph* earned him Columnist of the Year honours.[5]

And in 2008 he snagged both the GQ Politician of the Year and the coveted Brylcreem Best Celebrity Hairstyle awards.[6]

---

1 Purnell, Sonia. *Just Boris: Boris Johnson: The Irresistible Rise of a Political Celebrity*. (London: Aurum Press, 2011), pp. 176–8.
2 *The Times*, 23 Marc 2004, p. 10.
3 *The Times*, 13 April 2004, p. 6.
4 Gimson, p. 125.
5 *The Times*, 17 December 2005, p. 2.
6 *The Times*, 3 September 2008, p. 13 and 11 December 2008, p. 13.

32. BORIS BIKED INTO A LABOUR BROUHAHA

When Labour Party Leader John Smith died unexpectedly in 1994, Tony Blair and Gordon Brown made a famous deal. In return for Brown standing aside so that Blair could succeed Smith, the latter agreed to step down eventually to allow the former to replace him.[1] By 2004, seven years after Labour came to power in the 1997 general election, relations between the two had become tense as Brown grew impatient for Blair to cede power as promised. Into the breach biked Boris Johnson.

In early June, a month after Deputy Prime Minister John Prescott prompted speculation about Blair's future by discussing the succession with Brown at an oyster bar, *The Spectator* published an article that that added fuel to the fire. It purported to detail a conversation between Jonathan Powell, Blair's chief of staff, and Boris Johnson, the magazine's editor, that had transpired when the two men met by chance at a traffic light in Westminster while cycling home. Talk quickly turned to the sticky issue of the Labour leadership, with Powell telling the MP for Henley that Brown's desire for the top job was like a Shakespearean tragedy. 'Gordon Brown is like the guy who thinks he is going to be king but never gets it,' Powell reportedly said. He added that Blair would serve a full third term, but said he had advised his boss to be frank and admit that he could not commit to serving a full fourth term. In response to the article, Downing Street denied that Powell had made the remarks attributed to him: 'There was some light-hearted banter on Pall Mall but the last person Jonathan would confide his innermost thoughts is to Boris.'[2]

Although Johnson insisted that the story was 100 per cent accurate, explaining that he had written down the details of the

---

1 'Gordon Brown Admits to Leadership Deal with Tony Blair,' 12 February 2010, bbc.co.uk.
2 'Boris rides into row of Labour succession,' by Ben Russell, 4 June 2004, Independent.co.uk.

conversation immediately afterwards, others were not so sure. Powell's partner, Sarah Helm, told a Johnson biographer that the MP had put words in her man's mouth: 'It was a fantastic Boris-esque example of a story being half-way there but not standing up.' The biographer, Andrew Gimson, concluded, 'As with so many of Boris's stories, one could say that while the details were dubious, the general drift was right.' Even if the story was accurate, there was a question of the propriety of repeating a conversation conducted under those circumstances. Johnson conceded to an interviewer that he had some qualms about possibly traducing 'the fraternity of cyclists' but ultimately concluded, 'it was a jolly interesting story.'[3]

---

3 Gimson, p. 182.

33. BORIS SUPPORTED THE IMPEACHMENT OF TONY BLAIR

Impeachment, first employed by the Good Parliament of 1376, originally was one of the few mechanisms by which the Lords, and later the Commons, could hold ministers of the Crown accountable. The innovation did not exactly take off: it was used only once in the fifteenth and sixteenth centuries.[1] The procedure gained renewed life in the seventeenth century as Parliament sought to use it to rein in the Stuart monarchs. The next century saw one of the most famous and drawn-out impeachment cases when, over the course of seven years, Warren Hastings, former Governor-General of India, was impeached but ultimately acquitted of corruption charges. The last attempted use of the process came in 1846, when the Commons voted against impeaching Lord Palmerston, who had been accused of having received money from the Tsar in connection with the signing of a secret treaty with Russia.

So it was rather unexpected when Welsh nationalist MP Andrew Price announced his intention in August 2004 to impeach Prime Minister Tony Blair for 'high crimes and misdemeanours' in making the case for the war with Iraq. Even more surprising, Price sought advice from Matrix, a legal practice co-founded by Blair's wife, Cherie Booth QC, and received support not only from a handful of Welsh and Scottish nationalists MPs but also from three Tories, including Boris Johnson.[2] That Blair's conduct had already been officially examined four times, without uncovering evidence that he had misled Parliament or the country or wilfully distorted intelligence findings, only added to the sense that the move to impeach was little more than a quixotic stunt by MPs frustrated by Parliament's inability to stand up to the Prime Minister.[3]

---

1 Brown, A. L., 'Parliament, C. 1377-1422', in *The English Parliament in the Middle Ages,* ed. by R. G. Davies and J. H. Denton (Manchester: Manchester University Press, 1981), p. 140.

2 *The Times*, 27 August 2004, p. 2.

3 The Times, 28 August 2004, p. 29.

Had the Commons supported impeachment, the PM would have been arrested by the Serjeant-at-Arms, who would then have transferred the prisoner into the custody of Black Rod in the Lords. Blair likely would have been granted bail before his trial began in Westminster Hall, with the Lords serving as jury and a number of MPs serving as counsel for the prosecution.[4]

That, of course, was never likely to happen, which is why the impeachment bid was derided as 'probably the silliest story to emerge over the summer'. The Commons, where the Labour Government held a huge 159-seat majority, was never going to back the move. Indeed, Speaker Michael Martin was thought highly reluctant even to allow such a motion, particularly given that in 1999 a parliamentary committee had concluded that the power of impeachment 'may be considered obsolete'. That Johnson, who had supported the war, was now willing to lend his support to such a futile, but sensational, effort, seemed a testimony to his hunger for publicity.[5] The owners of *The Spectator* reportedly were 'appalled by Johnson's judgment' when he used his position as editor of the supposedly Thatcherite magazine to back the impeachment attempt.[6]

---

4 'Impeachment in Practice,' 2 September 2004, BBC.co.uk.
5 *The Times*, 28 August 2004, p. 14.
6 *The Times*, 2 September 2004, p. 6.

34. BORIS IS COOL (AND FUN AND WITTY)

That, at least, was the conclusion of the marketing company Superbrands, which came up with a list of the coolest people and brands of 2004. Johnson earned a spot by being innovative, original and true to himself, according to company chairman Stephen Cheliotis, who added, 'People like Boris Johnson because, quite simply, there isn't anybody else quite like him. And because he's funny.'[1]

Compilations of this sort tend to evoke controversy over who makes the cut and who does not, as well as jealousy on the part of those deemed unworthy of inclusion. That Johnson was the only politician seen to make the grade prompted speculation of envious rivals in Westminster Palace: 'Peter Mandelson and Michael Portillo must be gnashing their teeth – all that fastidious grooming, ignored in favour of a man who looks like a binbag of discarded clothes shuffling along to the charity shop under its own steam.'[2]

Perhaps predictably, not everyone in 'Cool Britannia' thought the Tory MP for Henley deserved a place in the pantheon containing such icons of style and hipness as Jonny Depp and Sir Richard Branson. When *The Times* (itself designated as 'cool') asked readers if they agreed with Johnson's selection, the response was mixed, as was the logic. One responded that Boris is 'Cute, cuddly, comical, candid even, and, of course, Conservative, but cool? No. Warm, more like.' Another doubter asked tellingly, 'If Boris Johnson is so cool, why has his novel failed to dent the bestseller lists?' Yet many others begged to differ. One reader argued, 'There is no one cooler in politics' (perhaps not the highest bar imaginable) than the MP who regularly cycles to work. A second fan was even more effusive, designating Johnson 'truly and utterly the coolest man alive', perhaps 'because he looks utterly startled' or 'because of his unruly hair, which looks like a theatrical wig.' A third

1 *The Times*, 29 September 2004, p. 10.
2 *The Times*, 1 October 2004, p. 2 (S).

asserted that Johnson's willingness to hide his intelligence behind a 'mumbling and bumbling' façade is only possible due to an unthinkable amount of self-confidence. That is, after all, what cool is.' And yet another supporter made perhaps the most cogent point: 'There are few politicians, nay few people, who can boast a large following of schoolgirls as well as the affection of every viewer of *Have I Got News for You*.'[3]

Probably the definitive word, however, came from Darian Leader, a psychoanalyst and author, who argued that cool was paradoxical: once something has been designated as such, people flock to adopt it, making it uncool. Johnson, however, does the opposite. Instead of conforming to what others do, 'Boris embodies himself. Almost to caricature.' Indeed, he identifies with his own fundamental oddness to an almost narcissistic extent, rather than trying to hide it. Such self-sufficiency, or at least the appearance thereof, 'acts like a magnet', which is very cool.[4]

And 'cool' was not Boris's only accolade. A 2006 *Reader's Digest* poll named Johnson as Britain's second-favourite 'figure of fun' behind heavy metal singer Ozzy Osbourne.[5] The following year, in a survey of 3,000 people by a digital television channel, Johnson ranked thirteenth in a list of 'Britain's wittiest individuals'. Although that put him well behind Oscar Wilde, who claimed the top spot, it did make Boris the highest-ranking politician.[6]

3 The Times, 1 October 2004, p. 34.
4 *The Times*, 2 October 2004, p. 3 (S3).
5 *The Times*, 23 August 2006, p. 9.
6 *The Times*, 15 October 2007, p. 11.

35. BORIS WROTE THE NOVEL
SEVENTY-TWO VIRGINS IN 2004

According to one review, Johnson's 'parliamentary romp, in which terrorists and traffic wardens, dim MPs and an automaton American President are caught up in a bloody whirlwind in the course of five mad hours, is a satire that sometimes works and sometimes doesn't.' Johnson, who 'can't resist a joke in every second paragraph', sometimes seems as if 'a tidal wave of bad taste' is about to overwhelm him, but barely manages to stay afloat. 'Not since Alan Clark named his dogs after Hitler's mistress has a Conservative MP managed such an act, able to ridicule the War on Terror, the White House, the police, and the official mind itself, as it searches ceaselessly for the sock bomber, the pants bomber, the vest bomber, the Biro bomber, and – most rare and admirable – the bra bomber.'[1]

Another reviewer calls Johnson 'a heroic failure as a novelist', who nevertheless managed to mine for comic insight the ideological motivation of Muslim suicide bombers and the 'mixed blessing of the American empire'. Still, it seems Johnson 'has written a witty page-turner, but not quite a novel', a 'flight of fancy' of the sort found on the pages of the publications for which he writes, 'populated by cartoon characters and chatty bathos'.[2]

In light of both the author and events contemporaneous to the book's publication, the novel inevitably was seen as something of a roman à clef. The book's central character is Roger Barlow, 'a shambling, bumbling, bicycle-riding Tory MP who is worried that his moment of extra-marital madness is about to be exposed by a tabloid.' Johnson denies that he is Barlow, before telling an interviewer, 'But you've got to use what you know, haven't you?'[3] Then there is a scene featuring

---

1 *The Times*, 18 September 2004, p. 13 (S2).
2 'Drats. MP Falls foul of facts,' by David Smith, 2 October 2004, theguardian. com.
3 *The Times*, 11 September 2004, p. 46 (S4).

a nanny named Sandra throwing a huge egg at a diplomatic car. An ostrich named Kimberly had laid the aforementioned egg. Given that David Blunkett resigned as Home Secretary in late 2004 amid accusations that he help fast-track the renewal of a work permit for the nanny of his ex-lover, Kimberly Quinn, publisher of *The Spectator*, there was speculation that Boris Johnson was advising his boss to behave like a struthian by keeping her head down.[4]

More recently, following Johnson's political ascent, his 'terrible' novel has been analysed for what it says about the author's own views. After all, the fictional work of other novelist-politicians, such as Disraeli and Churchill, often shed light on the policies they would pursue in office. So, it is a concern that Johnson's novel is 'racist, sexist [and] fundamentally undiplomatic'. The French are portrayed as 'perfidious, duplicitous [and] imperially arrogant'. Perhaps more surprisingly, the book is 'relentlessly anti-American', a stance attributed to Johnson's support for prosecuting British Prime Minister Tony Blair for war crimes. In sum, 'few readers would seem likely to come to the conclusion that the author would or should subsequently become UK Foreign Secretary.'[5] But, of course, that is precisely the post that Johnson assumed in 2016.

---

4 *The Times*, 6 January 2005, p. 13.
5 'What does Boris Johnson's terrible novel *Seventy-Two Virgins* tell us about him?' by Mark Lawson, 17 July 2019, theguardian.com.

36. BORIS APOLOGISED TO LIVERPOOL

Soon after British civil engineer Kenneth Bigley was kidnapped and beheaded in Iraq in late 2004 there appeared on the pages of *The Spectator* an unsigned article arguing that Britain had lost all sense of proportion by honouring him more conspicuously than soldiers who had been killed while serving in that country. The 'extreme reaction' to Bigley's death was attributed, in part, to him being a native of Liverpool, 'a handsome city with a tribal sense of community'. Economic misfortune and 'an excessive predilection for welfarism' have created 'a peculiar, deeply unattractive, psyche', as a result of which many Liverpudlians 'see themselves whenever possible as victims, and resent their victim status; yet at the same time they wallow in it.' Typically, they try to blame others for their misfortunes, refusing to accept that they may have been at least partly responsible. Such was the case when more than 50 Liverpool football supporters died at Hillsborough, when scapegoats were made of the police and *The Sun* newspaper, inexcusably failing to acknowledge the role played by 'drunken fans at the back of the crowd who mindlessly tried to fight their way into the ground.'[1]

The author of the story eventually was revealed to be Simon Heffer, a leader writer for *The Spectator*. But Boris Johnson had come up with the idea of a piece decrying the 'mawkish sentimentality' of the British public in the wake of the death of Diana, Princess of Wales. And Johnson had commissioned the article. So, even though he did not write the essay, Boris accepted responsibility for it.[2]

So frenzied was the reaction to the piece that it seemed likely that Johnson would pay, at least figuratively, with his head. David and Frederick Barclay, owners of *The Spectator*, recently had purchased Littlewoods, a catalogue empire based in Liverpool. As a result, they were among the largest private

1 'Bigley's Fate,' 16 October 2004, spectator.co.uk.
2 *The Times*, 21 October 2004, p. 11.

sector employers in Merseyside. The brothers reportedly were outraged by the essay, which went down rather poorly with their staff. Coming not long after *The Spectator* backed a 'childish' attempt to impeach Tony Blair, the article was seen to be 'the final straw'. Johnson, it seemed, was 'doomed at *The Spectator*.'[3]

One of his other jobs also appeared in jeopardy. Conservative Party Leader Michael Howard, anxious not to alienate potential voters, ordered his Shadow Culture Secretary to visit Liverpool to apologise. This Johnson duly did, but the results were deemed less than satisfactory from all sides. After arriving, Johnson 'spent the evening at an undisclosed safe house as citizens and the national media were in hot pursuit.' The next day, he remained elusive, holding a few 'hasty' interviews with local media, 'with all timings to be kept last minute to throw his pursuers off the trail'.[4] Such efforts to ensure that he ate only a small helping of humble pie were not completely effective. On live radio Bigley's brother called Johnson a 'self-centred, pompous twit' who should quit public life. The visit was such a public relations fiasco, that Johnson 'left Liverpool looking more of a prat than when he arrived'.[5]

So, it was perhaps appropriate, and not entirely coincidental, that when Liverpool was named 2008 European City of Culture in 2005, Boris Johnson became a member of the all-party parliamentary group created to assist.[6]

---

3 *The Times*, 20 October 2004, p. 6.
4 *The Times*, 20 October 2004, p. 10.
5 *The Times*, 21 October 2004, p. 11.
6 *The Times*, 2 December 2005, p. 39.

37. BORIS IS HIGHLY AMBITIOUS – BUT TRIES TO HIDE IT

Sonia Purnell, who was Johnson's deputy at the Brussels bureau of *The Telegraph* before becoming his biographer, told his soon-to-be wife in 1992 that Boris was 'the most ruthless, ambitious person I have ever met.' Although most people at the time saw Johnson as 'a charming, if shambolic hack defined by a love of classical civilizations and a problem with detail', Purnell concluded, after working closely with him, that 'under a well-cultivated veneer of disorganisation lay not so much a streak of aspiration as a torrent of almost frightening focus and drive.' She suggested, in print, that he could be a future Prime Minister as far back as 2002.[1]

Andrew Gimson, another former journalistic colleague turned biographer, notes that as a small boy Johnson indicated he wanted to be 'the world king', and never has 'grown out of this ambition. He has simply learned to conceal it.' Don't let his dishevelled appearance and apparently laid-back demeanour fool you. 'You will never find a more ferocious competitor than Boris, driven on by that sense of insecurity, but also by what he himself has called, with the intention that we should presume he is merely joking, his megalomania. He was not born to ease and comfort, but to wage a ceaseless struggle for supremacy.'[2]

Typically, Johnson uses humour to make seem absurd the very notion that he might seek or be able to climb the greasy poll. Such was his star power that, even before he was elected MP for Henley, the odds on him becoming the next Tory leader were said to be 50–1.[3] Some MPs would have killed for such a chance. Yet a year later, having entered Parliament, Johnson sought to deflect a question about him becoming party leader thus: 'Don't be silly. There is not a remote possibility. Believe me I am a toenail, the lowest of the low.'[4]

1 Purnell, p. 4.
2 Gimson, p. 17.
3 *The Times*, 2 June 2001, p. 11.
4 *The Times*, 5 October 2002, p. 14.

The following year, Johnson said 'it's more likely that I'd be blinded by a champagne cork, decapitated by a Frisbee, or locked in a disused fridge' than become editor of *The Daily Telegraph*.[5] In a similar vein several months later he famously opined, 'My chances of being PM are about as good as finding Elvis on Mars, or my being reincarnated as an olive.'[6] And, somewhat more prosaically, on the occasion of his 40th birthday, Johnson said, 'As I survey my life at 40 I can say I have achieved more than I intended and my leadership and career ambitions are sated.'[7]

Not everyone was taken in. Reviewing Johnson's career success to 2004, Jonathan Rendall wrote, 'You don't do that by being a blundering sheepdog. You do it by being ruthlessly ambitious.' He continued, 'Don't be fooled. There is a Project Johnson, it is backed by some powerful people, and its aim is to get him to No. 10.' As a result, Rendall (a committed gambler himself) called the 50–1 odds a bookie gave him on Boris becoming Prime Minister 'an absolute steal'.[8]

5 *The Times*, 6 October 2003, p. 2 (S).
6 *The Times*, 18 June 2004, p. 2 (S).
7 *The Times*, 19 June 2004, p. 14.
8 *The Times*, 10 July 2004, p. 35.

38. BORIS OFTEN THINKS WITH HIS JOHNSON

Johnson has had two marriages, innumerable affairs, and fathered more children than he is willing to publicly disclose. Yet he does not come off as an insufferable cad. He generally treats people kindly. His indiscretions seem to stem more from a failure to control his impulses than from a disdain for their consequences. He once observed, 'Three minutes is a very long time to keep thinking pious thoughts. I have read that the average British male is incapable of keeping his mind off sex for more than three minutes.'[1] In this, as in so many areas, Boris seems far from average, for he seldom seems to pass up an opportunity for gratification.

This seems partly due to a sort of philosophical orientation. Boris tends to see life as something of a virility test. 'If he sees an attractive woman, his instinct is to try to make a connection with her.' He is ardent in his pursuit of a romantic interest and sincere in the sense that, when he says what he thinks will help him obtain his objectives, he believes what he says at the moment he says it. This fleeting sincerity is all the moral self-justification he needs.[2]

Power is an aphrodisiac, so while someone with Johnson's wit and charm might have seemed seductive in any event, his allure grew as he became increasingly prominent. As President of the Oxford Union, women already reportedly were throwing themselves at Boris. By the time he became an MP, the attraction, and his willingness to respond, seem to have grown immeasurably. As biographer Sonia Purnell points out, 'Boris has an almost Clintonesque ability to make the person he is talking to at any one time – male or female – feel special... So while he was five foot ten inches of goosey flesh, overweight, sweaty, and not classically handsome by any means, he was fast becoming one of Britain's most accomplished lotharios.'[3]

1 *The Times*, 7 January 2005, p. 2 (S).
2 Gimson, pp. 167–8.
3 Purnell, pp. 86, 269–70.

And even when he did not appear to be actively trying to bed someone, he often recounts seemingly innocent situations in almost embarrassingly lustful tones. In a book he wrote on his election as MP for Henley in 2001, for example, Boris describes a scene while awaiting the final results. He and his wife Marina 'hobnob with some media, including some BBC bigfoots. And there, floating among us like an epiphany, a goddess: in what must rank as the highest compliment I could be paid by the corporation that once sacked me for speaking with the wrong voice, we have Anna Ford. She is looking indescribably lovely.' She wants Boris to appear on the BBC's *Election Special*. They have to wait awhile for the signal that they are on the air. Johnson continues, 'I have plenty of time to observe her great beauty. After about ten minutes of solid gazing and waiting, by which time I am quite faint with admiration, a flicker of irritation crosses that lovely, heart-shaped face.'[4] Although the pair never made it on the air that night, Johnson's rhapsodic account of his encounter with Ford cannot have been easy reading for Marina, particularly given that she was present at the time.

Similarly, on learning to disco dance with Ulrika Jonsson, girlfriend of (then) England football manager Sven-Goran Eriksson, Boris enthused, 'It was a bit like a goddess descending from Parnassus or Olympus and instructing a goatherd in a key advance of civilization, such as bee-keeping or wine-making.'[5]

---

4 *The Times*, 1 October 2001, p. 4 (S).
5 *The Times*, 27 April 2002, p. 18 (S).

39. BORIS HAD A FOUR-YEAR AFFAIR WITH PETRONELLA WYATT

Soon after Johnson was named editor of *The Spectator*, it was reported that the magazine's deputy editor Petronella Wyatt was stepping down from that post. The move came not long after the publication had been forced to apologise after BBC chairman Sir Christopher Bland complained about the quality of an interview she had conducted with him. Although Wyatt was expected to keep 'some association' with *The Spectator*, her departure was seen to allow Johnson 'to mould a deputy rather more to his image'.[1]

Johnson's desperation to get to the top, and willingness to joke about it, were, for Wyatt, 'a perfect mixture'. It did not hurt that, like her late father, Boris 'delighted in causing consternation, or at least surprise, on social occasions where others were on their best behaviour.' Both men were, according to a friend of the Wyatt's, 'flamboyant, self-centred characters, very clever mountebanks, but what they've left behind is quite sparse.' It also presumably was important that neither Boris nor 'Petsy' were strong on self-restraint. 'They incline towards boldness and impetuosity, rather than to the careful weighing-up of risks.'[2] Not long after she stepped down as deputy editor of *The Spectator*, Wyatt began what would become a four-year affair with Johnson.

It seems clear that Wyatt, 'one of London society's better-known *femme fatales*', wanted and expected Johnson to leave his wife and marry her. She even used her column in *The Spectator*, 'Singular Life', to hint that she had other options. And at one point she became engaged to an American lawyer and moved to Rhode Island. But when Boris wanted her back, she returned. The lovers might have continued indefinitely had they not been so brazen. The problem was not Johnson's wife, Marina. She 'had been aware of the relationship for some time but had not

1 *The Times*, 13 December 1999, p. 16.
2 Gimson, pp. 163–4.

thought it much more than an annoying distraction.' She was, however, not amused when Boris suggested the Petronella join a family holiday. No, the problem came when journalists, for whom the affair had been an open secret, learned that Wyatt recently had gone to the hospital to abort the second child sired by Johnson.[3]

Initially, reports about the abortion were fairly circumspect, declining to name either Wyatt or Johnson. But as newspapers competed for a scoop about a prominent politician, the gloves began to come off. In November 2004 Simon Walters, political editor of the *Mail on Sunday*, interviewed Johnson and asked about the rumours. Boris denied having an affair with Petronella, dismissing stories to the contrary as 'complete balderdash' and, more memorably, 'an inverted pyramid of piffle'. Johnson's wife, Marina, kicked him out of the house both for embarrassing her by allowing the affair to become public and because it became clear that Boris had continued to see Petronella even after promising not to do so. He went to stay with Justin Rushbrooke, a friend from Balliol.[4] Wyatt, 'whose faith in Tory MPs clearly needs restoring', soon found a new beau in Conservative whip David Ruffley.[5] But the fallout from the affair was only beginning.

3 Purnell, pp. 257–61.
4 ibid., pp. 261–3.
5 *The Times*, 3 December 2004, p. 15.

40. BORIS WAS SACKED FROM THE TORY FRONTBENCH FOR LYING ABOUT THE AFFAIR

In 1998, Johnson had written a passionate defence of a politician's right to lie about his private life. In discussing US President Bill Clinton's affair with aide Monica Lewinsky, Johnson argued that not only is it ludicrous to think that a man who lies about sex is untrustworthy but that exposing the affairs of politicians is only motivated by prurience and jealousy. So it may not be surprising that when asked about his relationship with Petronella Wyatt by Guy Black, spokesman for Tory Leader Michael Howard, Johnson denied they had had an affair. For a few days, it seemed that Boris would escape professional punishment. At *The Spectator*'s Parliamentarian of the Year lunch, held on 11 November 2004, a few days after Johnson's denial, Howard's remarks suggested that he was content to see Boris mocked in public without feeling a need to dismiss him from his spot on the front bench. However, Howard already had been unimpressed by Johnson's limited dedication to his parliamentary duties. So when, not long thereafter, more details emerged about the sordid tale, Howard sacked Boris.[1]

Johnson was 'undoubtedly chastened' by the experience. 'His front-bench career seemed to be over, virtually before it had started. If, as Henry Kissinger once noted, "power is the ultimate aphrodisiac", then Boris perhaps found that his sexual magnetism not quite "weapons grade" any more.'[2] Johnson's subsequent claim that he had not lied to Howard (apparently because he had not spoken to him directly) and his expression of hope that he could recover from the debacle 'further infuriated the party leadership, who were forced to pulp hundreds of conference programmes' for an event that was to have been headlined by the former Shadow Arts Minister.[3]

---

1 Gimson, pp. 211–3, 222–3.
2 Purnell, p. 272.
3 *The Times*, 16 November 2004, p. 6.

There were problems on other fronts as well. In the wake of his sacking there were reports that Johnson was fighting to keep his position as editor of *The Spectator*. Sir Frederick and Sir David Barclay, the devoutly Roman Catholic new owners of the magazine, were said to be 'at the end of their tether' with Boris, who not only combined the editorship with other activities but also drew attention to the publication for all the wrong reasons.[4] The subsequent appointment of Andrew Neil as the first chief executive of the magazine was seen as indication that Johnson 'has been put on probation' by the Barclays. Neil, evidently sent in as 'a minder for Boris', indicated that *The Spectator* was 'looking for a period of quiet'.[5]

So it is perhaps not surprising that Boris seemed a little stressed in the weeks following his dismissal. While presenting awards at a meeting of the Chartered Institute of Management Accountants, he was asked for his political hero. His response: 'it's the Mayor in *Jaws*. The one who kept the beach open.' That this led to some people becoming shark bait apparently was not the point. Rather, Johnson clarified, 'You should have the courage to stand up to events and not sack people for it.'[6]

A few months later, he made a similar point, if a tad more subtly. After Howard Flight indicated that if successful in the 2005 general elections, the Conservatives could make bigger spending cuts than they had promised during the campaign, Michael Howard withdrew the party whip and took steps to prevent Flight from being reselected by his constituency. Johnson dubbed the Tory leader 'Ming the Merciless'.[7]

4 *The Times*, 15 November 2004, p. 7.
5 *The Times*, 17 November 2004, p. 31.
6 *The Times*, 27 November 2004, p. 72.
7 *The Times*, 1 April 2005, p. 2.

41. BORIS GENERATES DRAMA

If the personal and professional fallout from his affair were not enough, it also exposed Johnson to ridicule. The man who often seemed to try to get people to laugh at him had inadvertently achieved it in a way he would not have chosen. It may have been cold comfort that he was not alone. The Tory leadership was widely mocked for sacking him over a private matter, particularly as Michael Howard had begun a romantic relationship with his future wife while she was married to someone else. But most of the derision appeared directed at the salacious goings on at the magazine Boris edited.

In addition to his affair with a colleague, columnist Rod Liddle was cheating on his wife with a receptionist, and publisher Kimberly Quinn was betraying her marriage vows with both Home Secretary David Blunkett and journalist Simon Hoggart. Boris and his merry band of adulterers at what wags came to call *The Sextator* became the subject of not one but two plays and a film.

In *Who's the Daddy*, a traditional farce, *The Spectator* is portrayed as an 'upmarket seraglio' and Johnson is a 'Blimpish buffoon with hair like a windswept haystack hiding under a bed on which a man and a woman are frolicking.' A smirking Michael Howard tells Boris that both he and the Tory party will prosper 'if they come across as firm upholders of family values. He doesn't realise that he's asking Priapus to become a bishop.' Soon thereafter, Johnson's character 'strips to his leonine pants and has it off with that spoiled shopaholic and palpitating sexpot' Petronella.[1]

The play's authors, Toby Young and Lloyd Evans, wrote theatre reviews for *The Spectator*, whose editor, Johnson, was a chum from Oxford. When they told him about their thespian endeavour, Boris wrote back, 'I always knew my life would be turned into a farce. I'm glad that the script has been entrusted to two such eminent men of letters.' Although he never saw

---

1 *The Times*, 27 July 2005, p. 17 (S).

the play in person, Johnson reportedly 'felt deeply hurt by it. He took to telephoning Young, begging him to scrap the projected transfer to the West End (which never came off) and telling him that his life had become "purgatory". Yet he gave no public expression to his distress, and did not sack either Evans or Young.'[2]

Johnson also declined to attend another play in which he was featured, *David Blunkett: The Musical*, telling Ginny Dougary, who wrote the script, that he had a 'pressing prior engagement'.[3] That's too bad because when he was photographed jogging in a 'skull-and-crossbones beanie and long baggy camouflage shorts, she knew just how to depict him: "Clearly behind that P. G. Wodehouse façade there was an urban rapper bursting to break free."'[4]

Johnson's sexcapades with Petronella even earned him a bit part in a film, *A Very Social Secretary*, which portrays Home Secretary David Blunkett as 'a love-struck buffoon'. It depicts Boris and Quinn conspiring 'to trap the 'simple Northern lad' in a high-society web that he is incapable of negotiating.' When Boris asks about Blunkett's sexual performance, Quinn replies, 'He cares too much about power. He's just a horny middle-aged man who wants a quick servicing before his red boxes.' The pregnant Quinn and Johnson then 'swap odds on who the father of her child might be'. Blunkett reportedly was considering legal action over the film, 'if it could affect the welfare of his two-year-old son with Mrs Quinn.'[5]

2 Gimson. pp. 232–3.
3 *The Times*, 15 April 2005, p. 34.
4 *The Times* 13 April 2005, p. 4 (S).
5 *The Times*, 6 October 2005, p. 36.

42. BORIS 'THE IDIOT' HELD HENLEY IN THE 2005 GENERAL ELECTION

As the General Election of May 2005 approached, Tory Leader Michael Howard had a problem. Boris Johnson, for all his gaffes and scandals, was perhaps the party's strongest electoral asset, but his unpredictability also seemed to make him a serious potential liability. To minimise the downside, Boris would have to be kept on a tight leash. 'A senior member of the Conservative Central Office staff during the election recalls specifically being told to "keep Boris out of the picture".' 'It was very tightly controlled,' he recalls. 'Boris's quotes were to be kept to a minimum.' A very senior Tory (who now advises him) was just one who simply dismissed Boris at this point as an 'idiot'.[1]

One place that Boris was given a bit freer rein was in Teignbridge, a constituency that adjoined the Johnson family farm. Stanley Johnson was seeking to wrest the seat from Liberal Democrat Richard Younger-Ross, who won it with a majority of 3,011 in 2001, and by so doing become the first father to follow his son into the House of Commons.[2]

The propinquity between apple and tree soon became evident. Andrew Gimson, a Boris biographer, witnessed the pair in action in Teignmouth in late April. 'Boris was wearing a suit with no tie and a modest blue rosette, while Stanley's rosette was a good six inches across.' Johnson *père* sought to persuade Johnson *fils* to perform 'a short walkabout in the rain, for the benefit of the considerable number of journalists who had come to watch. Boris was not keen and said: "Sod the press". A few minutes later he denied point-blank to me that he had said this.'[3] It did not help that Stanley's election literature misspelled the constituency's name. And that the aspiring parliamentarian wrote on his blog, 'If anyone asks me what I am planning to do

1 Purnell, p 276.
2 *The Times*, 31 July 2004, p. 12.
3 Gimson, p. 230.

in Westminster if I am lucky enough to be elected, I shall reply: Not too much I hope.'[4]

Accompanying the candidate in Henley, meanwhile, gave the impression that one has become 'trapped in a P.G. Wodehouse novel,' according to Ben Macintyre. 'Boris was on his best Bertie Wooster form yesterday, surrounded by an air of calculated vagueness, chaotic hilarity and canny, half-disguised ambition.' Approaching a man cleaning his caravan with a toothbrush, Boris asked if he would vote Conservative. 'No way, Jacko,' was the reply. 'Right-ho,' said Boris. 'Jolly good. Carry on toothbrushing.' As we departed Boris observed to nobody in particular: 'I think that went VERY well.' Following a few similar encounters, Macintyre concludes, 'Boris is a delight to go campaigning with: irreverent, unpredictable and bursting with self-irony. All qualities that endear him to the voters and terrify the party leadership. He simply cannot resist finding the funny side.' Voters evidently felt the same way, for many of them 'simply started laughing on seeing his tousled form'.[5]

For all the fun in his constituency, Boris evidently resented being kept on a leash, complaining, 'The trouble with campaigning in the wilds of Oxfordshire is that you lose touch with the main battle. I feel as if I'm lost in the jungle, way up the Nong River, 75 clicks beyond the Do Long bridge.'[6]

Boris would retain Henley with an increased majority of 12,793 while Stanley fell to Younger-Ross in Teignbridge by 6,215 votes.[7]

4 *The Times*, 23 April 2005, p. 39.
5 *The Times*, 19 April 2005, p. [23].
6 *The Times*, 4 May 2005, p. 2 (S).
7 Gimson, p. 232.

43. BORIS SUPPORTED DAVID CAMERON FOR THE TORY LEADERSHIP

The Conservatives gained 32 seats in the 2005 General Election, but Tony Blair's Labour Government retained power with a reduced parliamentary majority. In the wake of this disappointing result, Michael Howard resigned as Tory leader. Soon thereafter, Ladbrokes offered odds on who would succeed him, including David Davis (evens); David Cameron (5–1); Liam Fox (12–1) and Ken Clarke (10–1). The odds (100–1) of Boris Johnson replacing the man who had sacked him for lying about his affair with Petronella Wyatt were not the worst on offer; that dubious honour went to Howard's predecessor, Iain Duncan Smith at 150–1.[1]

Johnson had no intention of standing. Boris 'was far too canny not to appreciate that such a short, junior and accident-prone stint on the front benches was hardly a fitting qualification for throwing his own headwear into the ring. "My hat is firmly in my sock drawer, where it will remain," he quipped.' Instead, Johnson joined more than a dozen other MPs at a secret meeting in Portcullis House to pledge loyalty to Cameron. And, when Cameron dithered about whether or not he should stand for the leadership, Boris was one of the MPs 'pressing hardest' for him to do so.[2]

The support of Johnson and others was something of a mixed blessing for Cameron. Like him, many of his early backers (such as Boris) had gone to Eton or another prestigious public school. Downing Street disparaged Cameron's campaign team as 'Toffs on tour'. To counter such elitist aspersions, Cameron, 'the leader of the Notting Hill set of affluent young Tory thinkers, describes himself as a resident of North Kensington, an area known for ethnic markets and drugs, to try to create some street cred.'[3] It presumably was not lost on Boris that

---

1 *The Times*, 13 June 2005, p. 6.
2 Purnell, pp. 283–4.
3 *The Times*, 22 June 2005, p. 14.

whatever his own potential liabilities, he had been far more successful in finessing his privileged background as an issue: 'Far from denying his toffishness, he played up to it in such an amusing way that hardly anyone held it against him.'[4]

By September, Cameron's campaign appeared doomed. 'It had so far failed to attract much Parliamentary support; there were even suggestions from some MPs that he should "go away".' But Cameron's official launch on 29 September was far more successful than that of Davis, the frontrunner. Sensing the tide turning toward his man, Boris told the *Independent*: 'I am backing David Cameron's campaign out of pure, cynical self-interest.' A few days later, at the Tory Conference in Blackpool, Cameron 'delivered a career-changing performance that would define his image as a modern Conservative'. Cameron would become the new party leader, but Johnson's satisfaction at backing the right horse was tempered by dismay that he had been overtaken by a younger, less famous and less experienced public performer. This prompted a *Telegraph* article in which Johnson subtly portrayed his rival 'as an over-praised unknown, who had stolen ideas from the far more deserving Boris – as well as his rightful job.'[5]

The relationship did not improve much over time. In *Cameron: The Rise of the New Conservative*, published in 2009, Francis Elliott and James Hanning interviewed an associate of both politicians who asserts that Boris 'despises Mr Cameron, does not respect his intelligence, and cannot understand how he got the top job. Mr Cameron, for his part, sees Mr Johnson as being dangerously spirited and lacking the necessary moral cut-out or alarm system to be a serious politician.'[6]

---

4 Gimson, p. 237.
5 Purnell, pp. 284–5.
6 *The Times*, 25 April 2009, p. 5.

44. BORIS RESIGNED AS EDITOR OF *THE SPECTATOR* IN LATE 2005

It is almost hard to believe that Johnson survived as editor of *The Spectator* for six years. Conrad Black, the magazine's owner, had offered Johnson the position in July 1999 on the condition that he drop his parliamentary ambitions. Yet only a few months later, it became clear that Johnson had sought selection to be the Tory candidate in not one but two constituencies, leading Black to characterise Boris as 'ineffably duplicitous'. Not for the last time, Johnson apologised, conceded that Black would be well within his rights to sack him, and boldly asked to continue to serve as editor while also standing to become an MP. Black didn't want to lose Johnson, who he was counting on to raise the magazine's circulation, so he agreed.[1]

However, a year later, there were rumours that Johnson was 'already set to quit' as editor to focus on his political career,[2] and that 'pressure grows on Boris Johnson to relinquish' the editorship, although The *Spectator*'s publisher, Kimberley Fortier (later Quinn), indicated, 'at this time … there are no plans to replace Boris.'[3]

Two years hence, there was speculation that Johnson 'may have to choose between politics and journalism'. Black again was expected to put Boris on the horns of a dilemma. Under Boris's editorship, *The Spectator* 'has had more success attacking the Government than the parliamentary Tory party which Johnson occasionally deigns to represent.' Black, who also owned *The Daily Telegraph*, was thought to be considering Johnson for the newspaper's editorship. Were such an offer to be made, Johnson was expected to face a choice: editing a weekly magazine while serving as an MP was just about acceptable, but there would be 'an outcry' if he attempted to edit a daily newspaper while retaining parliamentary office.[4]

---

1 Purnell, pp. 189–90.
2 *The Times*, 28 July 2000, p. 23 (S)
3 *The Times*, 26 August 2000, p. 20.
4 *The Times*, 20 August 2002, p. 6.

And, when it seemed clear that Sir David and Sir Frederick Barclay would buy *The Spectator* and *The Telegraph* from Black, it seemed that Boris's days as editor of the former were numbered. 'The brothers, particularly renowned for their hard work ethic, prefer their editors to be full-time rather than part-time, like Mr Johnson.'[5]

In the end, the choice was forced upon Johnson not by the magazine's owners but by David Cameron. On the back benches for a year after being fired by Tory Leader Michael Howard, Johnson was eager for a frontbench role. Cameron, who was expected to become the new Tory Leader in late 2005, was willing to make his fellow Old Etonian a shadow minister, but only on condition that Johnson drop his editorship of *The Spectator*. The MP for Henley's acquiescence was thought to bring to a close 'one of the most colourful soap operas in recent Westminster history'.[6] As if. Soon after Boris resigned as editor in early December 2005, Cameron appointed him Opposition spokesman for higher education, a move that had been predicted by *The Times* a month earlier but 'almost immediately, rubbished by Mr Johnson'.[7]

5 *The Times*, 19 June 2004, p. 14.
6 *The Times*, 16 November 2005, p. 16.
7 *The Times*, 10 December 2005, p. 9.

45. BORIS BECAME SHADOW HIGHER EDUCATION MINISTER

If Johnson expected his 'pure, cynical self-interest' in supporting David Cameron for the Tory leadership to pay off handsomely, he was soon given cause to reconsider. When, in early December 2005, Cameron named his shadow cabinet, Boris's name was conspicuously absent. 'This was a humiliation, for which his appointment the next day [as shadow higher education minister] was scant compensation. Cameron had given his colleague a highly appropriate portfolio, but had also cut him down to size,' all the more so because Johnson had had to resign as editor of *The Spectator*.[1]

Johnson's new post was 'definitely a step up' from his previous frontbench role. And he took it more seriously too, forgoing the spoof manifesto he had released on becoming shadow arts minister the year before. 'His appointment was widely welcomed, as it seemed to suggest the Conservatives wanted to give the important question of higher education more prominence than it had previously warranted.' Although he supported the Labour Government's policy of top-up fees, he distanced himself from the previous Tory policy of cutting the number of university places. He also took back his own previous criticism of less traditional courses of study. During the 2005 election he had mocked 'loony degrees in windsurfing from Bangor University'. Now, apparently realising that this position would not win Conservatives any votes from those involved with those courses, he averred, 'My instincts are not to go around trying to exterminate Mickey Mouse courses. One man's Mickey Mouse course is another man's *literae humaniores*.'[2] However, those concerned about an erosion of standards would not have been reassured when Johnson's staff sent out a press release entitled 'Lecturers Pay Dispute' (*sic*) and referenced 'student's exam papers (*sic*).[3]

1 Gimson, p. 243.
2 Purnell, pp. 290–1.
3 *The Times*, 17 May 2006, p. 14.

BORIS JOHNSON IN 100 FACTS

Perhaps understandably, given his background, Boris seemed far more passionate about his higher education brief than he ever had about arts and culture. Criticising the decline of lectures in *The Times Higher Educational Supplement*, he wrote, 'It is human contact that gives students inspiration, and no wonder the current cohort sometimes feels uninspired. The hungry sheep look up and are not fed.'[4]

Several months later, he could not resist revisiting a pet peeve. Presenting at the National Television Awards, Johnson saluted all who work in or watch daytime television, which, he asserted, 'supplies a vital intellectual curriculum and a platform for the many indispensable courses in media studies with which this nation is so richly endowed'.[5]

Interviewed in the Cambridge student newspaper shortly thereafter, Johnson apparently made a dig of a more personal nature. 'We have a system in this country,' said Boris, 'whereby the elite, the rulers, avail themselves of selective education, either by having the economic power to move to an area by a good school, or by using fee-paying education, or by pretending to be religious and going to a church school.' When asked whether he had been referring in the last instance to David Cameron, who not long before had indicated that he was sending his daughter to a Church of England school, Boris replied, 'No. No. Goodbye.'[6]

---

4 *The Times*, 28 February 2006, p. 2 (S1).

5 *The Times*, 1 November 2006, p. 31.

6 *The Times*, 15 March 2007, p. 13.

46. BORIS WAS NOMINATED TO BE RECTOR OF THE UNIVERSITY OF EDINBURGH

Soon after resigning as editor of *The Spectator* and becoming Shadow Minister for Higher Education, Boris had the opportunity to take on another role. In January 2006 more than 275 students at the University of Edinburgh nominated him to be the school's next Rector. That this was more than eight times the number required was, according to the nominee, 'an encouraging start'. His competitors included Green MSP Mark Ballard, and two journalists, John Pilger and Magnus Linklater. Initially, all was sweetness and light. 'So far it's been terribly gentlemanly,' Johnson recounted early on, 'a sickening tide of harmony.'[1]

Then the gloves came off. Magnus Linklater entitled his *Times* column, 'Lend me your Xs or you'll get Boris.' He defended this 'naked abuse of editorial freedom' by pointing out that Johnson was the front-runner, with his face on posters around campus and regularly on television, and 'claims to be a Shadow spokesman for higher education'. Even worse, 'He's been out clubbing with the students and had beer poured over his head, which must be worth a couple of hundred votes.' Linklater promised that if elected Rector, he would not only try to bring more money to the university but also resist the trend to ask students to sign contracts obligating them to attend lectures. Although he declaimed any 'intention of playing the Scottish card', it was clear to everyone that 'Boris is, among other things, irredeemably English,' and is often found in London, whereas Linklater resided in Edinburgh. Perhaps most devastatingly, he concluded, 'you can find me at my campaign headquarters – the Blind Poet pub in West Nicholson Street – where pledges of support will be rewarded in the usual way.'[2] Linklater also provided a picture of Johnson wearing a Tam o' Shanter (and apparently ear muffs) as he allegedly tried to blend

---

1 *The Times*, 19 January 2006, p. 15.
2 *The Times*, 1 February 2006, p. 19.

in with the locals, asking 'Is this really the image that one of the greatest universities wants to project in its rector?'[3]

The Edinburgh University Students' Association, which traditionally did not get involved in rectorial elections, made an exception for this one. Angered by Johnson's support of top-up fees, it launched an 'Anyone but Boris' campaign. 'Posters were distributed urging students to "Practice Safe X – Don't Wake Up With a Dumb Blonde Tomorrow."'[4]

In the end, both campaigns appear to have been telling. Ballard won the contest with 3,597 votes. Linklater came in second, with 3,052. And Johnson finished third, with 2,123.[5]

Boris was gracious in defeat, praising both the victor and 'a very enjoyable campaign fought with tact, honesty and discretion'. Although he appeared to have snatched defeat from the jaws of victory, his self-assessment was rather different. 'Given I am English, a Tory and broadly in favour of top-up fees, this was a commendable performance.'[6]

3 *The Times*, 16 February 2006, p. 14.
4 Gimson, p. 248.
5 *The Times*, 17 February 2006, p. 2.
6 Gimson, p. 249.

47. BORIS IS A TACKLING DUMMY

In 2006 a charity football match was held in Reading before 15,000 spectators. The aim was to commemorate England's victory over West Germany in the finals of the 1966 World Cup. This time, the result was different: Germany won 4–2. But perhaps the most memorable aspect of the game was the play of Boris Johnson, who was 'running around like a demented combine harvester and tackling like a prop forward'. Wearing the No. 10 shirt, which may have said something about his political ambition, Johnson did not enter the match until the result was beyond doubt. But when he did take to the pitch, with 8 minutes remaining, the crowd 'cheered his every move'. When the ball went to Maurizio Gaudino, Boris launched himself at the former German international, 'in a style more appropriate to Twickenham'. As a rugby tackle it was not bad. 'The sight of the mop-haired MP for Henley's head powering into his stunned opponent's groin brought a roar from the crowd.' Afterwards, Johnson insisted his actions had not been malicious. 'I was going for the ball with my head, which I understand is a legitimate move.' However, he acknowledged that he had not played football since age 18, and before that it had only been on the beach or in the park, rather than in more formal settings. As a result, in the charity match, he said, 'I felt an enormous sense of achievement every time I actually touched the ball.'[1]

Almost a decade later, Boris made headlines again with another clumsy tackle. To promote a new health report, Johnson, by now Mayor of London, appeared with a group of schoolchildren playing football. As the ball rolled past, Johnson lunged for it, tripping a 9-year-old boy in the process. The youth, unfazed, quickly returned to the game while Johnson held up his hand in apology.[2]

1 'Great tackle, Boris – but it's football, not rugby,' by Bob Fenton, 4 May 2006, telegraph.co.uk.
2 'Boris Johnson "fouls" boy in children's football match,' by Georgia Graham, 15 October 2014, telegraph.co.uk.

And, in what may seem a fusion of the previous two mis-tackling incidents, there was a third embarrassing episode. In 2015, the Mayor of London went to Japan to promote trade. In Tokyo, he was invited to join a group of young boys on a mini pitch for a non-contact game of rugby. Boris, a keen rugby fan, seems to have lost the plot a bit. In the course of the match, Johnson got the ball and started running up the wing. There he encountered 10-year-old Toki Sekiguchi, who reached out to touch Johnson, and thereby stop play according to the rules of the game. Instead of stopping, however, Boris lowered his shoulder and ploughed forward, sending Sekiguchi toppling. The youngster subsequently indicated that he 'felt a little pain' from the encounter. The Mayor of London quickly apologised and shook the boy's hand. Afterwards the pair posed for photographs as Johnson gave Sekiguchi a 2015 rugby ball.[3]

---

3 'Boris Johnson knocks child to ground in touch rugby,' 15 October 2015, bbc.com.

48. BORIS HAS A WAY WITH WORDS

In fact, Johnson has something close to his own personal word: bemerded, meaning covered in excrement. It does not appear in the *OED*. The word apparently has been used only once in *The Times* (in 222 years), in a translation of *Rabelais*, and on a few other occasions. Mostly, as Ben Macintyre observes, Boris has made it his own. 'He has used it to describe the streets of Brussels, the streets of England, the streets of Islington and the Oxford cell floor where he spent the night after an evening boozing with the Bullingdon Club.' As a signature word, it certainly is well suited to Boris, 'being at once slightly risqué in an antique way, gently self-mocking, and also rather clever'.[1]

It's not just that he has his own word; he strings together those that are more widely used quite proficiently as well. His dismissal of suggestions that Britain's participation in the Iraq war might make terrorist attacks more likely was sardonic, if not prescient: 'In the restaurants of London, we are invited to imagine that Levantine waiters will sidle up and sprinkle anthrax on our spaghetti.'[2]

Many of his more memorable quips concerned, not surprisingly, the Labour Prime Minister. In mid-2003 he predicted, 'Mr Blair will not hold a referendum on the Euro or any European question, because he is a great quivering jelly of terror.'[3] When the Prime Minister was questioned by the leader of the Opposition a few months later, Johnson described the encounter thus: 'He wriggled before Michael Howard like a kebabbed witchetty grub.'[4] After the Hutton Inquiry cleared the Government of wrongdoing in the lead-up to the war, Johnson said of the Prime Minister, 'He is a mixture of Harry Houdini and a greased piglet. Nailing Blair is like trying to pin jelly to a wall.'[5] And, several months later, he predicted

1 *The Times* 28 July 2007, p. 16 (S3).
2 *The Times*, 21 March 2003, p. 2 (S).
3 *The Times*, 24 May 2003, p. 2 (S).
4 *The Times*, 12 January 2004, p. 2 (S).
5 *The Times*, 30 January 2004, p. 2 (S).

the Prime Minister was unlikely to resign soon. 'It is not in the nature of politicians to surrender their own political lives; they are like wasps in jam jars. They buzz on long after hope is gone.'[6]

On the eve of the 2005 general election, Johnson had what some interpreted as a dig at his boss, the Tory leader, who had forced him to make a humiliating visit to Liverpool. 'A victory for Howard would be a stunning vindication of his courage, resilience, patience, powers of organisation and penchant for spasmodic acts of apodictic ruthlessness.' He continued that Howard 'has imposed discipline on the good old principle of *Oderint dum metuant* [Let them hate me as long as they fear me].'[7] Soon thereafter, when the election returned Labour with a reduced, but still substantial, majority, Boris sought to put a hopeful spin on the result. 'This election was not a landslide for Tony Blair... What we are now seeing is the slow, sad political extinction of Tony Blair.'[8]

And the following year, during debate on the emergency extradition to the US of three bankers accused of fraud, Johnson accused the Blair Government of succumbing to American pressure, telling the Commons, 'We poodled. What? No, it's a verb. It is a noun, but it is also a verb. We did poodle. We poodled.'[9]

6 *The Times*, 30 April 2004, p. 2.
7 *The Times*, 6 May 2005, p. 7.
8 *The Times*, 6 May 2005, p. 9.
9 *The Times*, 13 July 2006, p. 10.

49. BORIS WAS NOT SACKED FOR ANOTHER ALLEGED AFFAIR

Soon after Johnson was appointed shadow higher education minister, Anna Fazackerley of the trade journal *Times Higher Education* called him the Conservatives' 'most popular and irrepressible' politician. She breathlessly continued that while he 'is not known for his discretion' he did display an impressive fluency with educational statistics before concluding, 'It is clear that those expecting controversy will not have long to wait. Mr Johnson has arrived. Let the show begin.'[1]

And begin it did a few months later when *News of the World* put Johnson on its cover with the assertion that he had been 'enjoying a series of secret trysts' with the 29-year-old Fazackerley. The credibility of the claim was vitiated somewhat when the tabloid later contended it had caught the pair sharing a hotel room in Paris, only to backtrack as it became clear that the woman in question had been Johnson's wife.[2]

There was considerable circumstantial evidence that Johnson and Fazackerley were having an affair, but both refused to confirm it publicly. Boris, it seemed, had learned at least a little from his past mistakes. 'This smart move allowed doubts to creep in that this was not an affair but merely a series of meetings to discuss education policy. After all, it was a patch they both patrolled, in their different ways.' Still, the fallout was considerable. Marina reportedly began wearing her wedding ring on her middle finger and, after finding her house besieged by reporters, filed a grievance with the Press Complaints Commission. Wyatt, whom Johnson had reportedly resumed seeing while also meeting Fazackerley, was said to feel 'heartbroken and betrayed'. And while David Cameron resisted calls to dismiss Johnson from his front bench, David Willets, the shadow education secretary, and therefore Boris's boss, was said to be 'narked' that his subordinate had lied to him about

1 Purnell, pp. 290–1.
2 Gimson, pp. 255–6.

the affair. More broadly, the episode 'undoubtedly added to Tory fears that Boris was a loose cannon and a lightweight'.[3]

The following year, Johnson's lenient treatment led to accusations of double standards. In late May 2007 Graham Brady announced that he was stepping down as the Tory Europe spokesman amid indications that he would be dismissed in an impending leadership reshuffle. He had angered Cameron by defending grammar schools. But some in the party felt Brady's transgressions were no worse than Boris's. 'They believe that Mr Johnson's gaffes are tolerated because he is closer to Mr Cameron. After all, they go to the same dinner parties,' a well-placed Tory source said.[4]

Fazackerley faced the most obvious consequences. Rumours of a relationship with Boris were seen to compromise her perceived impartiality. Her editor removed her from the politics beat. Although Boris later had lunch with the editor, evidently to try to dissuade him, 'the paper's management felt she had lost the confidence of her readership.' Shortly afterwards, Fazackerley resigned, but her new notoriety made it difficult to find work. Eventually she managed to find a job at a new think tank with links to Johnson, who, it seemed, was behind her appointment. But that must have been rather limited comfort given the Hell she went through due to her association with him, so Johnson's biographer asks why she, or other women linked to Boris, do not 'kiss and tell'. He concludes: 'Fazackerley's experience suggests they ask themselves who would fare worse if they did. The answer to that question is not Boris.'[5]

3 Purnell, pp. 298–9.
4 *The Times*, 30 May 2007, p. 2.
5 Purnell, pp. 300–1.

50. BORIS GOT INTO A 'FOOD FIGHT' WITH DAVID CAMERON

When Conservative leader David Cameron opened the party's 2006 conference in Bournemouth, he made social responsibility a principal theme. As an example, he pointed to Jamie Oliver's campaign for healthier school meals. This message was vitiated somewhat when Johnson, the Tory higher education spokesman, declaimed on the erosion of liberty at one of the conference's fringe meetings two days later. Boris said, 'If I was in charge, I would get rid of Jamie Oliver and tell people to eat what they like. But I would ban sweets from schools.' He further expressed support for two mothers in South Yorkshire who were reported to be delivering pies, fish and chips and fizzy drinks to as many as sixty students who desired alternatives to the healthy options on the school menu, saying, 'Why shouldn't they push pies through the railings?' When word of these remarks spread, Johnson 'was mobbed by a scrum of photographers, camera crews and reporters.' Evidently realising the embarrassment he had caused his party's leader, Boris backtracked, saying he supported Jamie Oliver, whom he thought 'a wonderful guy' and 'a saint'. His previous remarks had been misinterpreted. What he really believed was that schools should ban packed lunches so that healthy dinners would be the only option. 'I am an out-and-out paternalist. What I said was, let them eat liver and bacon, or whatever, healthy things like that... The point I am making is, provided that they don't have any option, they will eat it and it will be good for them.'[1]

His attempted revisionism does not seem to have helped much because his comments diverted attention from Cameron's keynote address to the conference. According to a biographer, 'top Tories were furious that Boris's remarks were overshadowing his leader's carefully crafted speech. He had created a good deal of resentment and anger.' Although Cameron subsequently

1 *The Times*, 4 October 2006, p. 29.

joked that Johnson had 'put his foot in it' and insisted that he was not upset his subordinate had gone 'off message', 'the Tory leader was obviously infuriated because he had not been given the clear media run he wanted.'[2]

Others were upset, but for different reasons. A letter to *The Times* two days later asked, 'When is Boris Johnson going to learn to stand by what he says?' The correspondent argued 'the electorate can appreciate individuals who put their head above the parapet and say the unthinkable, however unpopular.' So it was disappointing that Johnson did not 'challenge this new culture of health fascism'.[3]

Those on the Government benches were rather chuffed. At Education Questions a week later, Johnson earnestly spoke about physics teaching before sitting down. As Ann Treneman observed, 'When Boris isn't moving, he looks like a human-sized pudding topped with way too much coconut. Not a healthy sight.' Education Minister Parmjit Dhanda then taunted him about his comments in support of passing chips and burgers through the school fence. Boris claimed he was misquoted. Dhanda then pointed out, 'very smugly', that Oliver 'had already approved Labour's five-point healthy schools plan'. Another minister added, 'We continue to have conversations with St Jamie about his concerns and we always enjoy addressing them fully, unlike some.'[4]

2 Purnell, p. 305.
3 *The Times*, 6 October 2006, p. 22.
4 *The Times*, 13 October 2006, p. 38.

51. BORIS DREAMT OF ROME

In early 2006 Johnson presented a two-part series, *The Dream of Rome*, on BBC 2, following it up a month later with a book of the same name. Both 'displayed Boris at his best. Enthusiastic, funny and inspiring, he used all the senses, startling comparisons between ancient and modern – and of course, sex – to educate through entertainment.' Yet there also was evidence of other, less positive, Johnsonian traits. For, 'whatever the flashes of fun and ingenuity, there was also a flick of laziness, a sense that the book at least had been rushed. There are key details missing, arguments not fully backed up with facts.' Not surprisingly. After complaining to a colleague that it was 'bloody hard work, this book thing,' Boris was asked how long it had taken him to complete it. 'Bloody hell, two weeks!' was the reply.[1] He earlier lamented that the book was killing him, having written 14,000 words in three days.[2]

The reviews were mainly positive, with the main criticism being that Johnson sought to mix pleasure (his love of things classical) with business (an ideological message). Labour MP Denis McShane, concluded 'The odd attempt to link a marvellous reader-friendly account of Rome with an old-fashioned anti-Europeanism does not work,' partly because 'The EU, with 25 baleful national governments insisting on their sovereign rights is about as close to the Roman empire as any parish council' in Johnson's constituency.[3]

Another reviewer found it 'mostly convincing' even though key factors that promoted Roman identity and unity – the personality cults promoted by emperors and the sometimes forcible mixing of nationalities, 'like a gigantic Moulinex' – hardly seem applicable to the problem of EU integration.[4]

1 Purnell, pp. 292–3.
2 *The Times*, 15 December 2005, p. 15.
3 'The Dream of Rome,' by Denis McShane, 10 February 2006, independent. co.uk.
4 'Empire Building,' by Alex Clark, 4 February 2006, theguardian com.

More scathing was Tom Holland, himself author of a popular history of ancient Rome. Johnson sees 'the Roman Empire as both a model and a reproach to the modern-day EU,' but Mussolini tried to resurrect ancient Rome, an approach that has no appeal to Eurocrats. On the contrary, 'The Roman Empire should properly be regarded as the archetype of everything that post-war Europe has sought to avoid.' Equally 'lunatic' was Johnson's claim that the Empire's first two centuries AD provided a fiscal and regulatory model for Brussels. In reality, that period 'ended up a free-marketeer's worst nightmare: a despotism of blood and iron, with galloping inflation, high taxes and, yes, whole armies of bureaucrats.'[5]

While Boris was dreaming of Rome, others were dreaming of Boris. When two Belfast sixth-form classics students were unable to obtain tickets to his sold-out talk on Rome at the Oxford Literary Festival, they sent Johnson a letter, addressing him as *euplokame Boris, tu singularis victutis civis* [O Boris of the beautiful hair, thou citizen of outstanding virtue] imploring that he assist *nos per posticum firtim importando* [by smuggling us in the back door]. He responded by leaving tickets for the girls at the box office and when they subsequently introduced themselves, leaping 'to his feet with a resounding *Salvete*!'[6]

Johnson sought to enhance his own empire with a sequel, *After Rome: Holy Wars and Conquest*. It was less successful than its predecessor and tainted by scandal. To increase his financial take from the programme, Johnson secretly lured the director of *The Dream of Rome* to a rival production company, which Boris had set up, thereby cutting out the firm that had made the series. 'Boris was later found guilty by the Parliamentary authorities for failing to register his shareholding.'[7]

---

5 'Friends, Romans and Salarymen,' by Tom Holland, 19 February 2006, telegraph.co.uk.
6 *The Times*, 30 March 2006, p. 13.
7 Purnell, p. 294.

52. BORIS CHAMPIONED ANCIENT HISTORY

In early 2007 the OCR exam board, the only body offering an A level in Ancient History, announced it was dropping the subject in favour of a new Classical Civilization qualification. Johnson, who was not only the Tory higher education spokesman but also president of the Joint Association of Classical Teachers, asserted that it was 'demented' for the board to replace 'a tough, rewarding, crunchy' subject with a softer course of study. Classical Civilization would focus more on how historical periods were depicted in the literary record. Johnson lambasted this approach, arguing, 'You might as well say that you can learn English history through the study of the English language and literature. If we lose Ancient History A level, we lose yet another battle in the general dumbing down of Britain.' Others echoed Johnson's objections, pointing to a revival of interest in ancient history as reflected both in blockbuster movies and BBC documentaries and in a 300 per cent increase in the number of students studying the subject since 2000.[1]

A month later, the topic provoked a bit of class warfare during Education Questions. According to parliamentary correspondent Ann Treneman, the proposal had left Johnson 'the Dulux sheepdog in a suit' in 'a complete state.' He 'cannot stop referring to it. It is like a highbrow form of Tourette's.' Standing at the dispatch box, Johnson asked the Secretary of State for Education if he agreed it would be 'tragic' to scrap Ancient History A level because 'that will only intensify the dominance of a small number of schools in Latin and Greek classics and close down a potential route to university for children in the maintained sector that is potentially deeply regressive?' This prompted Dennis Skinner, the old class warrior, to reply 'Isn't it becoming increasingly obvious that the kids who are going to Eton school and are educated beyond their intelligence, like some of those on the

---

1 *The Times*, 31 March 2007, p. 25.

front bench, are being given additional opportunities to go to the posh universities while working-class kids don't get the same chance?'[2]

Two weeks later, Johnson donned a toga to accept a 4,000-signature petition calling for the retention of the Ancient History A level. The sixth formers from a school in Hammersmith who delivered the petition to the House of Commons were to conduct their meeting with the MP entirely in Latin. Prior to the encounter, Boris indicated that he already had been in touch with OCR and, while they were trying to come up with an acceptable solution, he was not very confident. 'I think they think that ancient history isn't a money spinner for them.'[3]

In late May OCR announced that Ancient History A levels would continue. It insisted that this was not backtracking; the plan to drop the exams had only ever been 'out for consultation' and 'never written in stone'. But the decision seemed a clear triumph for Johnson and others, such as Education Minister Lord Adonis, who had pushed the board to reconsider.[4]

2 *The Times*, 27 April 2007, p. 32.
3 'Boris joins the toga party for the cause of ancient history,' by Debbie Andalo, 14 May 2007, theguardian.com. *The Times*, 15 May 2007, p. 13.
4 'Cradle of Democracy,' by Jim Crace, 22 May 2007, theguardian.com.

53. BORIS INSULTED OTHER PLACES

In late 2004, Conservative leader Michael Howard sent Johnson to Liverpool to apologise for an article that had appeared in *The Spectator* that had referred to the city in disparaging terms. 'Operation Scouse-grovel', as the episode was termed, was not a roaring success, and would not be repeated (Fact 36). That is, perhaps, a pity, for it was not long before Boris was insulting not just other cities but entire countries.

On 7 September 2006, Tony Blair announced he would step down as Prime Minister within a year, ending prolonged speculation about when he would fulfil a promise made to Gordon Brown more than a decade earlier to cede power. That same day, Johnson wrote an opinion piece in *The Daily Telegraph* in which he stated, 'For ten years we in the Tory party have become used to Papua New Guinea-style orgies of cannibalism and chief-killing, and so it is with happy amazement that we watch as the madness engulfs the Labour Party.' This drew an immediate protest from Jean Kekedo, Papua New Guinea's High Commissioner in London, who pointed out that while the country had some problems with crime, it was a 'vibrant democracy' in which cannibalism and chief-killing were well in the past. There was a possibility that her government might declare Johnson *persona non grata* (being PNG-ed in the diplomatic argot). So potentially PNG-ed by PNG: a rare combination.

Boris responded that he had not meant to insult the country's people, 'who I am sure lead lives of blameless bourgeois domesticity in common with the rest of us,' adding, less helpfully, that the inspiration for his comments, a *Time Life* book from the 1960s, 'does indeed show relatively recent photos of Papua New Guinean tribes engaged in warfare, and I am fairly certain cannibalism was involved.' Kekedo then invited Johnson to visit her country to 'experience for himself the hospitality, kindness and genuineness of its people'.[1]

A few months later, reviewing in GQ the £340,000 Maybach limousine in which a chauffeur had driven the Tory spokesman on higher education to visit the University of Portsmouth, Boris lamented that its 'Poor bedraggled students splash across the campus in search of their lectures on feminism and media studies.' He went on to describe Portsmouth as 'one of the most depressed towns in Southern England, a place that is arguably too full of drugs, obesity, underachievement, and Labour MPs.' Mike Hancock, Liberal Democratic MP for South Portsmouth, replied that Johnson, 'a Tory toff who has no idea how people live in the real world', should be sacked from the Conservative front bench.[2] There was speculation that Operation Pompey Grovel might be necessary, for recent boundary changes had made the Tories competitive in the city's northern constituency.[3]

The following month, he did it again. After an 18-year-old student died after a golf society night out, Exeter University's Athletic Union banned its clubs from holding alcohol-fuelled initiations or drinking games. Interviewed in the student newspaper, Johnson compared the response to the prohibition of guns following the 1996 Dunblane massacre, saying, 'I am very much against panic bans as the result of some tragic incident... The Athletic Union should get a grip.' Anticipating the fallout from his comments, Johnson later said, 'I'm building up an unhealthily large portfolio of hostile towns rather quickly and I don't intend to add Exeter to my collection,' but his remarks hardly endeared him to local residents.[4] Indeed, reflecting on the ambit of his recent insulting comments, Boris later offered to undertake an 'apology world tour'.[5]

1 'Boris in hot water over cannibalism in Papua,' by Neil Tweedie, 9 September 2006, telegraph.co.uk.
2 'Now Johnson upsets Portsmouth,' by Stewart Payne and George Jones, 4 April 2007, telegraph.co.uk.
3 The Times, 4 April 2007, p. 13.
4 'Boris: Don't ban boozing,' by Geoff Maynard, 23 May 2007, express.co.uk.
5 Purnell, p. 296.

54. BORIS WROTE *THE PERILS OF PUSHY PARENTS* IN 2007

Boris and his siblings were pushed to be successful. 'From an early age, the family atmosphere was decidedly highbrow and literary: children's arts programme *Vision On*, story slot *Jackanory* and *Blue Peter* were the only TV programmes permitted. The Johnsons were BBC, rather than ITV children.' From age 4, Rachel was expected to read aloud leaders from *The Times*. 'Always, the need to achieve was thrust home.'[1]

So when Boris wrote a book of poetry entitled *The Perils of Pushy Parents* in 2007, it may have been aimed partly at his mother and father. If so, the message received may not have been quite the one he intended to send. A review in *The Guardian* doubted that 'a more cringe-worthy book has been published'. But the reviewer did acknowledge a smidgen of doubt. 'This year, an estimated 170,000 books will be published and, if I suggest this is only the 169,999th least worth reading, that is only because I am hedging my bets. A worse book might appear this year. It is a possibility.' The danger in question, according to Johnson, is that an outright ban on television is likely to have adverse and unforeseen consequences. So it is better to allow children screen time in moderation while also encouraging them to read. The problem was not Boris's message, or, as some argue that he spreads himself too thinly. Rather, according to the reviewer, 'He spreads himself too thickly, larding his unworthy crust with things that make it even more indigestible.' That is to say, 'he not only writes duff verse, he illustrates it too with inept drawings.'[2] Hardly a ringing endorsement for the product of the product of pushy parents.

---

1 ibid., p. 26.
2 'Behold them, reader, and despair,' by Stuart Jefferies, 9 November 2007, theguardian.com.

55. BORIS FOR MAYOR?

When a directly elected Mayor of London was proposed in 1997, Ken Livingstone, MP for Brent East, described the idea as 'absolutely barmy'. He would become the first to hold the new post after outpolling Conservative candidate Steve Norris in both 2000 and 2004. In the hopes of avoiding a third straight defeat, the Tories in 2006 sought to choose their candidate for 2008 by means of a primary in which all of London's registered voters would be eligible to participate. But after eight weeks of nominations, nobody deemed likely to provide much of a challenge to the popular Livingstone had come forward. Embarrassingly for the Conservatives, the selection process was postponed until the spring of 2007.[1]

From at least late 2005, Veronica Wadley, editor of *The Evening Standard*, had been trying to sell Tory leader David Cameron on a Johnson candidacy. 'But Boris, despite his popularity, was just not considered seriously.' By the spring of 2007, however, Cameron, who had taken personal control of the search, was getting desperate and the selection process was 'in danger of descending into farce'. After considering at least eight candidates, ranging from Lord Coe to Sir John Major, Cameron proposed to his Liberal Democrat counterpart, Sir Menzies Campbell, that their parties jointly support Greg Dyke, an idea that died as soon as word of it got out. Then, in early July, Nick Boles, the presumed candidate of last resort, announced he was pulling out of the race to seek cancer treatment. It appeared that the Tories might have to go once again with Norris, which did not seem a recipe for victory.[2]

By this point Boris had been 'urged again and again' by supporters to throw his hat into the ring, but 'was at first no more than cautiously keen'. With his safe seat and generally positive reviews as higher education spokesman, his parliamentary career appeared promising. However, on 2 July Cameron reshuffled

---

1 Edwards, Giles and Jonathan Isaby, *Boris V. Ken: How Boris Johnson Won London*, (London: Politico's, 2008), pp. 2, 13, 49.
2 Purnell, pp. 308–9.

his team, as a result of which Johnson was passed over in favour of more junior MPs such as Michael Gove. 'To be excluded from the Shadow Cabinet showed Boris he was going to get nowhere by playing the parliamentary game.' Becoming mayor, by contrast, could allow him to build a power base independent of David Cameron.[3]

Two days later Boris sort of, almost, threw his hat into the ring. As *The Times* reported, 'The twin farces of Boris Johnson and the search for a Tory London mayoral candidate collided yesterday as he was forced to issue a statement that he was not ruling himself out of the race.' After Cameron's office indicated that Johnson was 'definitely considering' entering the contest, Boris himself said, 'I'm definitely not a candidate.' But then Conservative headquarters issued a statement in his name indicating that Boris 'would consider the possibility very carefully'.[4]

Johnson's Hamlet-like indecision would continue until the last possible moment: he agreed to stand on the day nominations closed. Senior party officials quickly pared the dozens of nominees down to the five most promising. Bolstered by a poll that showed him defeating Livingstone by 6 per cent, Boris won almost four out of every five votes cast in the primary, becoming the Tory candidate for Mayor of London.[5]

3 Gimson, pp. 274–8.
4 *The Times*, 5 July 2007, p. 4.
5 Edwards and Isaby, pp. 52–3.

56. BORIS GETS A MAKEOVER

Johnson had momentum even before he became the official Tory candidate for Mayor of London. 'Supporters were said to be signing up to his campaign at the rate of 100 an hour through his website.' Ken Livingstone, the incumbent Mayor, made it clear that he expected his main rival to pose a formidable challenge, indicating that he was researching Boris by reading one of his biographies, which he called 'the scariest thing I have read since *Silence of the Lambs*.'[1]

The wheels soon appeared to fall off. Announcing his candidacy, Johnson delivered a speech 'more notable for its phrase-making than for its specific policy proposals'. Criticising Livingstone's dealings with Venezuelan leader Hugo Chávez, Boris said 'You won't catch me doing deals with left-wing dictators, which means that Venezuelan slum children are effectively subsidising Transport for London. I say that is completely Caracas!'[2] A week later he suggested 'the police were wasting their time by chasing cannabis smokers,' a position 'at odds with the Tories' zero-tolerance stance on drugs.'[3]

Perhaps more important than what he said was what he left unsaid. There was conspicuous silence from a man who previously had seemed unable to shut up. This was primarily because he was doing things other than campaigning. He was 'working on no fewer than three different television projects filmed in six different countries', writing his weekly column for *The Telegraph*, promoting a new book of verse, *The Perils of Pushy Parents*, while also performing some of the duties of an MP. 'It was almost as if he could not quite believe that he was running for mayor, or that it was worth his complete and serious attention.' It seems that, like many, he did not believe he could win but felt a good showing would help his career.[4]

1 *The Times*, 18 July 2007, p. 24.
2 *The Times*, 4 September 2007, p. 24.
3 *The Times*, 12 September 2007, p. 2.
4 Purnell, 317.

For Tory Leader David Cameron and his campaign chief George Osborne, Johnson's nonchalance was a concern. They saw the contest for London as a potential harbinger of Conservative fortunes in the next General Election. Osborne met with Johnson to urge him to make more of an effort, and tried to get him to take on Conservative Central Office staffer James McGrath, to no avail. Soon thereafter Cameron joked, 'Inside Boris there is a serious, ambitious politician fighting to get out.' The gag, while seemingly affectionate, was laced with menace.[5]

Soon thereafter, Cameron brought in Lord Marland, a wealthy businessman, to shore up the mayoral campaign's finances. And Lynton Crosby, the Australian political strategist nicknamed the 'Wizard of Oz' was drafted in to provide direction and focus. Crosby flew to meet Johnson after Christmas 2007. 'After years of indulgence and special treatment, Boris did not know what had hit him: he was informed he had to "lift his game" to avoid "letting down his team".' Later, Marland and Crosby took Boris to dinner. 'Talking softly but bluntly across the white linen tablecloth, the pair delivered a sobering message: he had to show commitment to winning. Losing, even by a tiny margin, was not an option.' This would mean hard work, self-discipline, punctuality, and avoiding further scandals. They ended the meeting with a warning: 'If you let us down, we'll cut your fucking knees off!'[6]

It was not long before 'new-look' Boris made his appearance: 'He is wearing a slick business suit, a perfectly knotted tie and has groomed hair. He is, most alarmingly of all, bang on time.'[7] The candidate had had a makeover.

5 *The Times*, 14 November 2007, p. 28.
6 Purnell, pp. 322–4.
7 *The Times*, 15 March 2008, p. 38.

57. BORIS WAS ELECTED MAYOR OF LONDON

At the start of 2008 Boris acknowledged that his London mayoral campaign to date had been, 'crap'. Yet a poll put him only 1 per cent behind Ken Livingstone, who was facing growing accusations of cronyism in office.[1] A Johnson victory, once seen as a near impossibility, had become plausible.

This seems to have motivated Boris to heed the advice of the campaign strategists that Conservative leader David Cameron had encouraged him to employ. The difference was soon obvious. Boris 'broke decisively with the self-destructive style of politics which he had learned from his father Stanley: the style according to which absolutely everything has to be treated as a joke and played for laughs, however seriously one may inwardly be taking it.' The gaffes that had been the source of such excited press coverage were greatly reduced. 'In their place was a grasp of policy which sounded the equal, in most respects, of Ken's, allied to a far greater determination to do something about questions – knife crime, children terrorising elderly people on buses – about which Ken seemed to have given up, or to have nothing new to say.'[2]

Lynton Crosby, in charge of organising Johnson's campaign, realised that Boris was seen as likeable and funny, attributes that often mattered more to voters than a politician's policies. So, while emphasising these assets, he pushed Johnson to deal effectively with potential criticisms. This meant drilling the candidate in how to rebut accusations that he was racist, homophobic or too posh for the job. And, to counter those who tried to dismiss Boris as nothing but a 'clown', sober policy proposals were developed. Crucially, these were aimed at appealing to residents outside central London, many of whom had not bothered to vote in previous elections. Improving public transportation, reducing congestion, planting trees

---

1 Edwards and Isaby, p. 84.
2 Gimson, pp. 282–3.

and cleaning up parks were elements of Crosby's 'doughnut' strategy. Nor did it hurt that Johnson's wife Marina, seldom seen in his parliamentary constituency, repeatedly appeared with him in London.[3]

The impact was not immediate. In mid-February *The Times* opined, 'The problem for the Tories is that, three months after entering the contest, Mr Johnson has not begun to campaign.' His failure 'to mount a credible challenge' to Livingstone 'risks becoming an embarrassment to the Conservatives and a disappointment to the capital'.[4]

However, little more than a month later, the newspaper reported that Prime Minister Gordon Brown 'has all but written off Ken Livingstone's chances of winning the London mayoral election, according to close allies'.[5]

In the month before the election, Johnson, who had given up drinking for the duration of the campaign, announced that if elected, he would ban the consumption of alcohol on the Tube.[6] A few days later, he proposed a one-off amnesty to illegal immigrants who had been in Britain for more than four years, a policy at odds with the stance of Cameron.[7]

Johnson's 1 May 2008 victory was symptomatic of a broader trend: local elections were a disaster for Labour, which lost 331 seats, its worst showing in four decades.[8] Having won more than 1 million votes (and 53.2 percent of the total cast), Johnson now had the largest single mandate of any elected politician in Britain. He promised not to revert to his former self. 'I was elected as New Boris and I will govern as New Boris, or whatever the phrase is,' he joked – in a rather Old Boris kind of way.[9]

---

3 Purnell, 326–30.
4 *The Times*, 15 February 2008, p. 16.
5 *The Times*, 27 March 2008, p. 14.
6 *The Times*, 3 April 2008, p. 15.
7 *The Times*, 7 April 2008, p. 25.
8 *The Times*, 3 May 2008, p. 1.
9 Edwards and Isaby, pp. 201, 204.

58. THE NEW MAYOR FACED A STEEP LEARNING CURVE

Johnson's early days as mayor 'would demonstrate all too publicly his woeful lack of preparation for the job – or understanding of it'. David Cameron and George Osborne had pushed Boris to revamp his campaign in late 2007, but for quite a while afterwards do not seem to have given serious consideration to what would happen in the seemingly unlikely event that he became mayor of London. Their neglect of the issue, combined with Johnson's lack of administrative experience and tendency to be easily distracted, meant that little attention was paid to who would staff the new administration should he prevail.[1] Indeed, days after he became mayor it was reported that, 'The search is on for the most senior and important members of Boris Johnson's new team.'[2]

Even worse, some of those eventually chosen for this team were compelled to leave it rather abruptly. James McGrath, Johnson's senior political strategist, was forced to resign in June over racially insensitive remarks. McGrath's comment that immigrant blacks could leave London if they did not like the Tory administration initially did not seem to threaten his job, but Johnson, with a history of questionable racial comments himself and a desire to underline his differences from former mayor Ken Livingstone, quickly decided his aide had to go.[3] Less than two weeks later, Deputy Mayor for Youth Ray Lewis, a key figure in Johnson's effort to reduce teenage knife crime, resigned amid allegations of sexual misconduct and financial irregularities. The incident was thought to be 'highly damaging' to Johnson, who had appointed the former vicar while pledging to run a cleaner regime than Livingstone's.[4] A month later, Johnson's administration 'suffered a severe blow'

1 Gimson, pp. 356–7.
2 *The Times*, 6 May 2008, p. 15.
3 *The Times*, 23 June 2008, p. 16.
4 *The Times*, 4 July 2008, p. 11.

when Tom Parker, whom Boris had recruited from the private sector to be his first deputy mayor and chief of staff, quit only weeks into the jobs after clashing over the scope of his responsibilities.[5]

If Boris may be forgiven for a bit of organisational ineptitude, some of the other problems of his early days as mayor were more of his own making. He 'got off on the wrong foot with staff at the Conservative Party's headquarters after barring them from his victory party'.[6] A few months later there was 'no sign of the new, organised Boris Johnson', when the mayor, the guest of honour at a dinner given by the Board of Deputies of British Jews, arrived 'breathlessly late', after having forgotten the formal attire demanded by the occasion.[7]

Boris did have form in this regard. In his first week as mayor, he was late to two official functions. One of these was a meeting with Prince Charles, when Boris arrived 'drenched in sweat and over half-an-hour late after boarding a Tube travelling in the wrong direction whilst being mobbed by a group of middle-aged London-Chinese women (and not noticing for several stops)'. Nor was his reputation helped when, three weeks into a job at which he had promised to work 'flat out' Johnson swanned off to Turkey for a week's family sailing holiday. With a start like this it was perhaps no wonder that senior Conservatives, anxious that Boris not undermine the party's prospects in the next general election, began to distance themselves from the man in whose election they recently had found such inspiration.[8]

---

5 *The Times*, 20 August 2008, p. 8.
6 *The Times*, 3 May 2008, p. 3.
7 *The Times*, 17 July 2008, p. 13.
8 Purnell, pp. 366, 368.

59. BORIS'S CHINESE WHISPERS

As host of the 2012 Olympics, London's mayor was to attend the 2008 Beijing Olympics to formally accept the handover of the Games. Even before Boris became mayor there were signs that he might not treat the occasion with the dignity it demanded.

Asked whether he supported trampolining and BMX biking as (recently introduced) Olympic sports, Johnson indicated that he did, but proposed joining the two so that athletes would 'do BMX biking on trampolines'.[1] A month later, when told the mayor would have to attend the closing ceremony, 'Are you sure I have to go?' asked Boris, checking his diary. 'I'm supposed to be in France.'[2]

Johnson introduced a bit of austerity to the Olympic handover celebrations to save £1.2 million. This entailed cancelling a plan to send 18 Gordon Ramsay chefs to serve businessmen and politicians at the Games, flying economy to Beijing, and staying at a less expensive hotel.[3]

But Boris's attitude evidently soon changed. Those on the International Olympic Committee were sticklers for protocol, so Johnson was thought to be studying its guidelines to avoid 'national embarrassment'. His role in the ceremony was to receive the 6-metre Olympic flag, held horizontally, from his Beijing counterpart and then wave it back and forth exactly eight times. In early June that he claimed to have been 'practising daily' his flag routine, conscious that 'to drop it' in front of an audience estimated at 100 million would not do.[4]

Surprisingly, Johnson's big time gaffe in the run-up to the Beijing Olympics took place on his own patch. Appearing on the *Today* programme, Boris promised that the London Olympics would be the best since the first games were held in 753BC. A shocked fellow classicist quickly informed *The*

1 *The Times*, 19 February 2008, p. 4.
2 *The Times*, 18 March 2008, p. 24.
3 *The Times*, 13 June 2008, p. 4.
4 *The Times*, 16 June 2008, p. 9.

Times that the date the mayor cited was the traditional date of the foundation of Rome by Romulus; the first Olympics were held in 776.[5]

Another Johnsonian controversy appeared anything but a mistake. Writing in *The Telegraph*, Boris argued that the performance of British athletes in Beijing had shown as 'piffle' claims, made most notably by David Cameron, that Britain was 'a broken society in which the courage and morals of young people have been sapped by welfarism and political correctness.' The article prompted renewed speculation that Johnson might seek the Tory leadership, 'suggestions he did little or nothing to quell'. However, his subsequent actions at the closing ceremony hardly helped his case. Rather, 'his failure to button up his jacket while waving the flag in Beijing caused a mini diplomatic incident – offending his Chinese hosts and many older viewers, who thought him scruffy and disrespectful.'[6]

Johnson also 'drew hilarity from most of the world' by claiming table tennis was not invented in China, asserting, not entirely accurately: 'Ping-pong was invented on the dining tables of England in the nineteenth century and it was called whiff-whaff.'[7]

Johnson subsequently announced that 'there is no Olympic jacket-button protocol,' as he had checked with a relevant official. He had been tempted to button up, but 'then thought, sod it' and decided, 'to follow a policy of openness, transparency and individual freedom. No disrespect intended. It's just that there are times when you have to take a stand.'[8]

So, despite having picked up a new suit from a Chinese tailor for his star turn at the Paralympic Games in Beijing a few weeks later, 'there was Boris, unbuttoned, letting it all hang out again.'[9]

---

5 *The Times*, 20 June 2008, p. 35.
6 Purnell, p. 372.
7 *The Times*, 2 September 2008, p. 14.
8 *The Times*, 28 August 2008, p. 15.
9 *The Times*, 18 September 2008, p. 11.

60. BORIS EARNS 'CHICKEN FEED'

On the eve of Johnson's election as Mayor of London in May 2008 there was speculation that he might continue as MP for Henley for as long as a year.[1] However, little more than a month later, he was appointed Steward and Bailiff of the Manor of Northstead, a Crown office that disqualified him from sitting in the Commons.[2] (Accepting such an office is the standard way for MPs to leave Parliament voluntarily, since there is no mechanism for them to resign directly.)

The salary of an MP (around £80,000) is considerably less than that of the Mayor of London (around £140,000), so it might seem surprising that Boris was concerned that changing jobs could hurt his wallet. Yet days before the mayoral election he had confessed to Brian Paddock, a rival candidate, that should he win, 'I don't know how I'm going to manage financially.' Anxiety about money was a constant Boris theme, but in this case it evidently stemmed from a belief that he would have to give up his £250,000-a-year *Daily Telegraph* column, which he had suspended while campaigning for mayor. As it turned out, the paper's editor, unable to hire a viable replacement in the interim, was keen for Boris to resume his column. And City Hall authorities adjudged this to be 'no conflict of interest'. But Boris's decision to continue to write for *The Telegraph* infuriated his senior advisor, Nick Boles, who worried that it would foster the impression that the mayor was not fully committed to the duties of his office. Boles and other 'minders' therefore pressured Johnson to agree to donate a fifth of his *Telegraph* salary to charity. This concession reportedly left Johnson 'squealing with fury: "It's outrageous! I've been raped! I've been raped!"' Boris seems to have responded by donating to charity considerably less than he had promised.[3]

But not long thereafter, Conservative leader David Cameron asked members of his shadow cabinet to give up the second

---

1 *The Times*, 1 May 2008, p. 6.
2 *The Times*, 5 June 2008, p. 15.
3 Purnell, p. 260–2.

jobs by the end of the year. Asked about this on the BBC's *Hard Talk* programme, Johnson argued that 'Frankly, there's absolutely no reason at all why I should not knock off an article as a way of relaxation.' He went on to dismiss the money he received for the articles as 'chicken feed', adding, 'of course I make a substantial donation to charity.'[4]

Johnson's characterisation of his *Telegraph* salary led to calls for him to apologise for being 'out of touch'. The head of Unison, a major public sector union, accused him of being 'wired to another planet'. The Fire Brigades Union said that Johnson's 'chicken feed' equated to 'the annual salary of 10 firefighters and two fire apprentices'. The leader of the National Union of Journalists pointed out that its members working in London earned as little as £16,000 per year. A mayoral spokesman said Johnson had no intention of apologising for what 'was clearly not a serious remark'. He added that anyone pretending Johnson does not consider £250,000 to be a lot of money 'is quite clearly engaged in political mischief-making'.[5]

---

4 'Mayor's £250,000 "chicken feed"', 14 July 2009, new.bbc.co.uk.
5 'Johnson condemned for describing £250,000 deal as "chicken feed"', by Hélène Mulholland, 14 July 2009, theguardian.com.

61. BORIS ESCAPES CENSURE FOR ANOTHER AFFAIR

In May 2009 Johnson brought art consultant Helen Macintyre to City Hall as an unpaid consultant. Around the same time, she persuaded her boyfriend Canadian financier Pierre Rolin to contribute to the construction of a huge red metal sculpture, dubbed the 'Olympian Erection', which was commissioned for the 2012 London Games. Several months later, Macintyre gave birth to a daughter. Rolin, suspicious about the timing of the pregnancy and the baby's lack of resemblance to him, took a paternity test, and found that he was not the father. He ended his three-year relationship with Macintyre, publicly blaming Johnson. 'How could Boris take £80,000 off a Tory donor after sleeping with his live-in partner of three years and possibly father[ing] her child?' he ranted. 'He has no moral compass whatsoever!' Although neither Johnson nor Macintyre publicly confirmed the affair, Boris's wife kicked him out of the marital home.[1]

A standards panel subsequently ruled that by failing to disclose his relationship with Macintyre, Johnson had committed a 'minor technical breach of the code of conduct' but ruled that censuring him was not required.[2]

A bit more than two years later, the Appeal Court rejected Macintyre's legal action against a newspaper for naming Johnson as her daughter's father. The judge indicated that while Macintyre had not made public statements about the child's paternity, she privately had told people that it was Boris's. Moreover Johnson's 'reckless' extramarital behaviour, which had resulted in the births of two children out of wedlock, was of public interest because voters might reasonably use it to evaluate his fitness for office.[3]

1 Purnell, pp. 407–9.
2 'No censure for Boris Johnson over relationship with unpaid City Hall advisor,' by Hélène Mulholland, 15 December 2010, theguardian.com.
3 'Public has right to know about Boris Johnson's secret lovechild, court rules,' 21 May 2013, telegraph.co.uk.

62. BORIS WAS IMPLICATED IN CONTROVERSY OVER THE ARREST OF MP DAMIAN GREEN

In late November 2008, police investigating Home Office leaks arrested MP Damian Green. Reaction was intense, with William Rees-Mogg calling it – and the police search of the Conservative immigration spokesman's home and office – 'the most serious breach of the privilege of Parliament in modern times.'[1] Boris was similarly scathing, but, as London's Mayor and therefore Chairman of the Metropolitan Police Authority, quickly faced questions about his own behaviour.

Soon after he was informed that the police planned to arrest Green, Johnson reportedly sought to phone the MP. Almost 20 minutes elapsed between the time Johnson was told of the planned raid and officers managed to locate Green. Johnson could not have known about this delay. And if he did attempt to warn Green, that potentially was an offence under the 1977 Criminal Justice Act, which prohibits 'attempting to assist an offender or impede an arrest'. However, such was the furore over Green's arrest that Johnson's apparent meddling was not seriously investigated. However, another Johnson phone call to Green a few days later was the subject of an inquiry, which found that, while Boris had not breached mayoral codes of conduct, his decision to contact the subject of an active police investigation was 'extraordinary and unwise'.[2]

When the Commons' Home Affairs committee held an inquiry on the leaks in early February, its chairman, Keith Vaz, predicted that Johnson would be unable to attend due to 'more pressing matters', namely a major snowstorm that was causing transportation chaos in the capital. Availing himself of an opportunity to catch the committee not fully prepared, Boris went to Westminster anyway, by bike, of course. 'Just as an aircraft can evade incoming missiles by emitting strips of

---

1 *The Times*, 1 December 2008, p. 25.
2 Purnell, pp. 381, 383.

metal foil known as chaff, so Boris baffles inquiry by emitting a stream of badinage known as chaff.' This he preceded to do, deflecting questions both about his call to Green and his subsequent discussion of the MP's arrest with Conservative leader David Cameron. However, the following day Johnson took a more aggressive approach in a phone conversation with Vaz, complaining that he was 'unbelievably disappointed at the way my evidence is being treated... So fucking angry.' After a few more profanity-laced comments, he concluded that the inquiry was nothing more than 'Fucking smear tactics from the Labour Party'.[3]

It was not just Johnson's possibly illegal contact with Green that was questioned. The Mayor's public criticism of the police while an investigation was ongoing also raised eyebrows. The day after the raid, Johnson told Acting Metropolitan Police Commissioner Sir Paul Stephenson that he found it 'hard to believe' that police from the anti-terrorism unit had been used to arrest an MP 'for no greater crime than allegedly receiving leaked documents'. He went on to indicate that he had yet to see convincing evidence that the Met's action had been 'necessary and proportionate'.[4]

A few days later former Met Assistance Commissioner Andy Hayman asserted that his erstwhile colleagues were 'increasingly agitated' by how politicians, particularly Johnson, handled the Green affair. 'Boris Johnson was informed of the Green arrest in his position as chairman of the police authority but chose to react in the role of prominent Tory politician.' Continued political interference in police operations could, Hayman suggested, have serious ramifications. 'The next commissioner will think twice before pre-warning the mayor of any future sensitive operation.'[5]

---

3 Gimson, pp. 305–7.
4 *The Times*, 29 November 2008, p. 3.
5 *The Times*, 2 December 2009, p. 5.

63. BORIS WAS ACCUSED OF CRONYISM

Cronyism was one of the chief charges Boris made against incumbent Ken Livingstone in the 2008 London mayoral race, so it was rather awkward when many of the Johnson clan sought employment after their most prominent member took charge of the capital. 'They all wanted jobs in City Hall afterwards,' fumed a very senior Tory. 'The other Johnsons are like baggage who come with Boris everywhere.' His father Stanley pressed hard for the Environment portfolio. Younger brother Jo apparently sought to become the mayor's head of strategy. However, it soon 'was made clear that Boris would not be allowed to hire his family and turn City Hall into a mayoral version of the *Spectator*—or *Johnsonator*, as it was known at one point when so many Johnsons were writing for it.'[1]

That bullet dodged, another was fired the following year in the form of Veronica Wadley. As editor of the *Evening Standard*, Wadley had been an early and stalwart backer of Boris for mayor, running a number of articles on cronyism under Livingstone. So when Johnson sought to install Wadley as the head of the Arts Council for London in late 2009, Livingstone claimed this was a 'pay off' for her previous political support. In a letter to the Culture Department, Liz Forgan, head of Arts Council for England, complained that Johnson had not only failed to follow the proper nominating procedures but had chosen someone 'manifestly less qualified' than the shortlist's other three distinguished candidates. Culture Secretary Ben Bradshaw vetoed Wadley's appointment, arguing that it was in 'clear contravention' of the Nolan principles governing public appointments. Johnson, furious, criticised the decision as 'politically motivated' and vowed not to nominate another for the post until Bradshaw was no longer Culture Secretary.[2]

In the meantime, Johnson made a number of efforts to get around Bradshaw's ban, leading to considerable media

1 Purnell, pp. 358–9.
2 'Ken Livingstone claims Boris Johnson tried to "pay off" former Evening Standard editor,' by Hélène Mulholland, 9 October 2009, theguardian.com.

speculation about his motivations. The one that mattered apparently was not partisanship. 'Boris feared that if he failed to get her the job, Veronica would go on the warpath saying, "But I created you!"' explains a former colleague. 'The sense of payback had become acute. He was a little scared of her and even thought she had a crush on him – cracking jokes about her being Mrs Robinson in *The Graduate*.' Johnson's apprehension did not last that long, for in the General Election of May 2010 the Conservatives came to power. The following month Jeremy Hunt, the new Culture Secretary, appointed Wadley to the London Arts post.[3]

3 Purnell, p. 402.

64. BORIS BECAME A 'KNIGHT ON A SHINING BICYCLE'

In early November 2009, Franny Armstrong, a climate-change activist and filmmaker, was walking home in North London. Busy texting on her phone, she did not notice the approach of a number of hoodie-clad girls until they pushed her up against a car, 'quite hard'. One of the assailants was holding an iron bar, which made the encounter 'very frightening' to Armstrong. Spying a cyclist nearby, she called out for help. To the rescue rode Boris Johnson, Mayor of London, who just happened to by riding past. When he asked the girls what they were doing, they fled, dropping the iron bar in the process. Johnson, a large man who played rugby at Eton and Oxford, picked up the bar and set off in pursuit, calling the girls 'oiks' in the process. The mayor did not catch them, but he did return to Armstrong a few minutes later, after which he escorted her home.

She later conceded that, as the founder of the 10:10 campaign, which sought to reduce carbon emissions by 10 per cent by 2010, her political views were not in accord with those of her rescuer, whom she referred to as her 'knight on a shining bicycle'. Indeed, in the 2008 race for Mayor of London, she had voted for Johnson's main rival, Ken Livingstone. But, politics aside, she had to admit that, 'if you find yourself down a dark alleyway and in trouble I think Boris would be of more use than Ken.'[1]

1 'Johnson saves woman from 'oiks'', 3 November 2009, news.bbc.co.uk.

65. BORIS THE BUILDER

In his eight years as London's Mayor Johnson left an extensive 'built legacy'. Not only did the cost of the average home increase by 60 per cent but the period saw the construction of 'a series of whimsical follies' in architecture, public art, and transport, 'stunning not only for the shallowness of their conception, but also for the sheer fact that the unstoppable will of Johnson managed to make so many of them happen.'[1]

Often previously hostile to skyscrapers, Johnson became 'rather more pragmatic' after arriving in City Hall.[2] Indeed, his enthusiasm for all types of buildings evidently increased. 'The Crystal', a sustainability exhibition combined with an auditorium and office space, was symptomatic of Johnson's approach – encourage investors 'to put money into a project for which there was no real need, in exchange for branding and promotional opportunities', topping it up with public funding without much oversight.[3]

Johnson had oversized influence on London's built environment in part because of the construction boom related to the Olympics. Many of the structures created for the games, such as the Aquatics Centre, were beautiful. The ArcelorMittal Orbit is a conspicuous exception. Described variously as an artwork, viewing platform, visitor attraction and extreme entertainment venue, this 'cacophony of forms', a 400-foot high bright red tangle of tubes, 'was not part of the original Olympic bid, nor part of the masterplan. Its existence is almost entirely down to the efforts of Johnson, who conceived of the project, and muscled it into existence though sheer gusto and opportunism.'[4]

It was not just through the promotion of ostentatious, if not always terribly useful, projects that Boris reshaped London. His predecessor, Ken Livingstone, sought to address

---

1 Murphy, Douglas, *Nincompoopolis: The Follies of Boris Johnson* (London: Repeater, 2017), pp. 2–3.

2 *The Times*, 17 December 2008, p. 14.

3 Murphy, pp. 23–4.

4 ibid., pp. 37–40.

the capital's housing shortage by constructing tall tower blocks, an approach dubbed, 'build 'em high and damn the planners.' As new mayor, Johnson made clear his opposition to large buildings that obstructed historic views and pledged to shift the emphasis from flats to 'more family-friendly homes with gardens'. His planning advisor, Sir Simon Milton, was more explicit, 'This fetish for tall building will be a disaster for London.'[5]

In late 2008 Johnson proposed spending £5 billion to create 50,000 affordable homes. Moreover, noting that the average floor space of a London home was considerably smaller than other places, the new residences would be larger. Or, as Boris put it, 'I am not about building homes for Hobbits.' However, critics pointed out that with 750,000 people waiting for social housing in London, Johnson's plan provided the city's boroughs with little incentive to provide it.[6]

Before long, however, Johnson seems to have abandoned many of his reservations. Proposed developments over a specified size are automatically referred to the Mayor's office, so 'planning is one of the issues over which Johnson had a serious amount of power.' While he occasionally rejected planning applications, far more frequently he approved them, as recommended by local authorities. However on as many as 19 occasions he approved projects despite local objections about their scale, or perceptions that the developments 'seriously clashed with local heritage and historic urban fabric'.[7] Instead of simply wantonly approving new housing, as Johnson did, 'a better Mayor would have taken planning seriously, as more than just a rubber-stamping tool, in fact one capable of helping shape areas and spaces and communities for the benefit of more than just the shareholders of the developers and pension funds who pay for the towers to be built.'[8] Quite.

5 *The Times*, 23 May 2008, p. 23 (S1).
6 *The Times*, 21 November 2008, p. 25.
7 Murphy, pp. 164–8.
8 ibid., p.180.

66. JOHNSON COMMISSIONS BORIS BIKES

In mid-2007 Paris introduced a scheme, paid for with advertising revenue, to station thousands of bicycles around the city for the public to hire for short journeys. London's mayor, Ken Livingstone, considered a similar programme for the British capital, but lost office before he could implement it. His replacement, Boris Johnson, eager for a conspicuous success prior to seeking re-election in 2012, rushed to put the scheme in place (and directed City Hall staff not to mention Livingstone's role). The logistics of the project, from arranging a system of payments to determining the locations of docking stations to physically delivering the bikes and ensuring that the stations did not run out of them, were daunting. And at times it seemed that the result would be a catastrophic failure. But soon after the first so-called Boris Bikes hit the streets in July 2010 the programme was widely considered a success, at least from a political standpoint. The finances of the scheme were another matter. Although Johnson secured private sponsorship for the programme (including a pledge of £25 million from Barclays), this fell far short of meeting its costs. 'The middle-aged, affluent white males found to be the greatest users of Boris Bikes cleverly avoid paying for them (beyond the £1 access fee) by returning them within the 30-minute period granted for free.' Partly as a result, Transport of London estimated that the bikes could cost taxpayers £100 million over Johnson's first term as mayor.[1]

It was not just the overall cost that was problematic. The appeal of Boris Bikes seems to have varied considerably across London's demographic groups. 'The richest fifth of the population cycle on average 2.5 times as far in a year as the poorest fifth.'[2] Soon after becoming mayor Johnson announced that Tube and bus riders would face eight years of above-inflation fare increases, while at the same time cancelling

---

1 Purnell, pp. 414–6.
2 *The Times*, 21 September 2007, p. 3.

10 transport schemes in which the Livingstone administration had already invested £60 million.[3] So Johnson effectively subsidised a form of transportation favoured by the well-off while increasing the cost of getting around for others.

There also was a question of safety. Before becoming mayor, Johnson was publicly disdainful of measures that might save the lives of bicyclists. Weeks after his election, a newspaper published a photograph of a bare-headed Boris 'cycling through six red lights, riding on the pavement and not stopping at a pedestrian crossing'. A chastened Johnson apologised, and promised to wear a helmet, before adding, 'I can't promise it will be all the time.'[4]

It wasn't just that Johnson's flippant personal attitude was seen to encourage unsafe cycling. To promote Boris Bikes, while not supplying them with helmets, much less mandating that riders wear them, seems irresponsible. And to promote the use of the bikes without also taking steps to improve road safety for cyclists seems negligent. Indeed, it was only in 2013 that Johnson sought to address this issue by appointing a cycling commissioner and promising funds.[5]

One of his ideas was for a cycling superhighway on which those on bikes would be protected from traffic. Perhaps not coincidentally, the first Boris Bike fatality came that same year, when a lorry struck a young woman riding in an unprotected bike lane.[6]

---

3 *The Times*, 7 November 2008, p. 32.
4 'Boris: I admit I need to start wearing a helmet,' 13 May 2008, standard. co.uk.
5 Murphy, pp. 142–4.
6 'First fatal 'Boris bike' accident in London,' by Mark Townsend, 6 July 2013, theguardian.com.

67. BORIS INTRODUCED A NEW ROUTEMASTER BUS

In 2000 London Mayor Ken Livingstone said that 'only a ghastly, dehumanised moron would want to get rid of' the capital's iconic Routemaster buses. However, four years later, Livingstone reversed course, arguing that the double-decker buses, introduced five decades earlier, were no longer fit for purpose because, among other things, they were inaccessible to wheelchairs and large prams. In late 2005 almost all the Routemasters were withdrawn from general service, often replaced by articulated buses commonly known as 'bendy buses'. This change became an important topic in the 2008 mayoral election. Boris Johnson, the Tory candidate, claimed 'Bendy buses are miserable, inhuman and socialistic and should all be pensioned off to a Scandinavian airport.' He promised to phase them out and commission a new, improved Routemaster.[1] According to Andrew Gimson, Johnson's biographer, 'There can be no doubt that this was a highly popular thing to do.'[2]

Soon after riding that promise into City Hall, Johnson announced a competition, with a prize of £25,000, for ideas for a modern bus, with the stipulation that entries strongly resemble the Routemaster.[3]

Almost two years later, Johnson got behind the wheel of the engineering prototype of the new bus, which would produce 35 per cent less emissions than a comparable diesel vehicle and was produced 'almost entirely' in Britain. Typically, Boris waxed hyperbolic, if not necessarily credibly, on his new toy, 'I've driven Lamborghinis and Ferraris but this is the best. This is the smoothest. This is the most hi-tech piece of motoring technology I've ever seen.'[4]

1 *The Times*, 19 December 2007, p. 26.
2 Gimson, p. 307.
3 *The Times*, 5 July 2008, p. 35.
4 'Boris Johnson and the Routemaster: soft edges and cheerful demeanour,' by Zoe Williams, 27 May 2011, theguardian.com.

It should have been, for developing the bus, and purchasing the first eight cost a whopping £11.4 million. Partly for that reason, the future of the Routemaster appeared in doubt in advance of the 2012 mayoral election. Ken Livingstone, again the Labour candidate, promised to buy no more of the buses, which he deemed overly expensive.[5]

Soon after Johnson secured re-election as mayor, London ordered 600 of the new buses for £160 million. And because the Routemasters had been designed specifically for the capital, private operators evidently feared they would be unable to resell them after 10 years, as they typically did with London buses. This meant that Transport for London, that is, the taxpayer, had to buy them.[6]

Not long after Johnson left City Hall in 2016, Sadiq Khan, his successor as mayor, announced that he would buy no more Routemasters in order to fund a four-year freeze in public transport fares.[7]

Khan's decision was all the more poignant because Johnson's mayoral legacy was built on a few high-profile transportation policies. As with Boris Bikes, the advent of Boris Buses was not accompanied by related infrastructure improvements. While Johnson continued most of the transportation strategies inherited from Livingstone, he did little to continue his predecessor's efforts to bolster bus use. 'In the years after Johnson took office, the large increase in service provision for the bus network came to an almost complete halt, despite the continued increase in London's overall population.' Moreover, bus fares increased by two-thirds.[8]

---

5 'Ken Livingstone vows to halt rollout of new Routemaster buses,' by Hélène Mulholland, 18 April 2012, theguardian.com.

6 'London to get 600 new "Boris buses" – but taxpayers will foot the £160 million bill,' by metrowebukmetro, 20 September 2012, metro.co.uk.

7 'London's "Boris bus" reaches end of road as Sadiq Khan halts purchases,' by Daniel Boffey, 31 December 2016, theguardian.com.

8 Murphy, p. 146.

68. BORIS SUPPORTS LAW AND ORDER

Given Conservative claims to be the party of law and order it is perhaps not surprising that as a candidate for Mayor of London Johnson promised to take a harder line on crime than his Labour rival, Ken Livingstone. His manifesto pledged to increase policing on buses, which were seen to have experienced a surge in violence after Livingstone allowed youth to travel for free. Likewise, Johnson called for an alcohol ban on public transport as a means of improving order. But the main plank of his anti-crime platform was a pledge to assume the chairmanship of the Metropolitan Police Association, a post Livingstone had eschewed.[1]

So it was shocking when, hours after taking over as chairman, Johnson forced the resignation of Commissioner Sir Ian Blair, the top officer at Scotland Yard. To be sure, Sir Ian was unpopular, was alleged to have awarded contracts improperly to a friend, and had led a Met that was criticised for racial discrimination against senior Asian officers and, most notably, for the death of Jean Charles de Menezes, killed by armed police who had mistaken him for a suicide bomber. But Johnson had given no indication that he was upset with the commissioner's leadership, and had not bothered to inform Home Secretary Jacqui Smith, under whose jurisdiction the Met falls. Johnson's bold move, characterised in *The Times* as a 'Tory coup', also fuelled concerns within the police service about the growing influence of party politics.[2]

According to Andrew Gimson, 'This was the episode which established Boris as a serious player. The muzziness of the rules, and his acute sense of timing, had enabled him to dominate a transaction in which he ought to have been no more than a junior partner.' In doing so, he managed to anger Prime Minister Gordon Brown and show up Smith for failing to do 'the right thing' by sanctioning Sir Ian for his 'grotesquely

---

1 ibid., 215.
2 *The Times*, 3 October 2008, p. 1.

inadequate' response to the shooting of de Menezes. What is more, Boris deftly mended fences with the Home Secretary to agree on the next commissioner so that 'no lasting political wrangle was allowed to undermine the policing of London.'[3]

Yet some of Mayor Johnson's other moves were less adept, reminiscent instead of the Boris of old. While overall crime levels fell under his administration, as it had under Livingstone's, Johnson the candidate had promised to address violence against young people, in particular stabbings. He therefore resorted to a number of untruths. He claimed during Mayor's Question Time that 'serious youth crime is coming down,' when the Met's official statistics showed 'serious youth crime to have dramatically increased', with knife crime up by close to a fifth in two years. Likewise, his assertion that police numbers were increasing on his watch was hard to square with Met figures that 'indicated the exact reverse'.[4]

Then there was the mayor's apparent callousness or indifference to police misconduct. After police were criticised for the 2009 unlawful killing of Ian Tomlinson, a newspaper vendor, Johnson lamented, 'I worry that there are large sections of the media that are currently engaged in a very unbalanced orgy of cop bashing.' Two years later, the fatal police shooting of Mark Duggan prompted riots in London. Boris, on holiday in Canada, initially refused to come home, expressing confidence in the police. 'This decision not to come back was widely criticised, and by the evening of the third day of rioting he belatedly announced that he was returning.'[5]

---

3 Gimson, p. 304.
4 Purnell, p. 436.
5 Murphy, pp. 219, 232.

69. BORIS (MOSTLY) LIKES BANKERS

As Mayor of London, Johnson often sought to portray himself as a man of the people. One conspicuous exception to this generalisation was his treatment of bankers, who were not the most popular sorts in the wake of the financial crisis that began soon after Johnson became mayor. To be fair, he realised he needed them. As he told two interviewers, 'I'm a friend of the bankers but do not forget that this is a bankogenic recession. It wasn't produced by some oil shock, it was produced by a crisis in the financial services industry. The recession will be a lot worse than it need be unless the banks understand that they need to reach out and help small businesses.'[1]

Less than a year later, at the Conservative Party Conference in October 2009, Johnson did a bit more to indulge his 'relish for saying the outrageous'. First, he called for a referendum on the Lisbon Treaty, thereby undermining Tory leader David Cameron's position that such a vote was not practicable after the document had been ratified. After that particular act of defiance, Boris received a text in Italian from senior Conservative staffer Nick Boles, '*La vendetta è un piatto che va mangiato freddo,*' which means 'Revenge is a dish best eaten cold.' Then, having appealed to the populist wing of the party, Johnson moved in the opposite direction, telling the Conference, 'I know how unpopular these bankers are and I know how far out on a limb I now seem to be in sticking up for these pariahs. But never forget, all you banker-bashers, that the leper colony of the City of London produces 9 per cent of Britain's GDP and 13 per cent of value-added taxes that pay for roads and schools and hospitals across the country.'[2]

To be sure, Johnson was not averse to criticising bankers in general or in particular. A few months before his comments at the Conference, Boris had a go at Sir Fred Goodwin, the former chief executive of the Royal Bank of Scotland,

---

1 *The Times*, 6 December 2008, p. 31.
2 Gimson, pp. 321, 324.

who was to receive a £30 million pension despite having driven the institution into the ground through an aggressive acquisition policy. As a result, Goodwin had become, according to Johnson, 'the epitome of the bankers who collectively occupy a place in public opinion significantly lower than cannibalistic paedophile global-warming deniers'.[3] Nor were bankers the only targets of his sarcasm. After attending an international property development conference, Boris caustically commented, 'They say money can't buy happiness, and I can confirm this is entirely true. The economic outlook is dire, they bemoaned. There is no hope left, they muttered over their shoulders as they slinked off to their yachts and into the night.'[4]

But while Boris occasionally referred to bankers as 'scum' or 'tossers' and spoke of the 'deep public rage' their actions had evoked, insiders reported that he spent much of his time as mayor 'schmoozing' with them either on the phone or in person. Despite Johnson's rhetorical backing for victims of knife crime, those affected by Tube breakdowns, the homeless, the downtrodden, etc., these 'have not earned such energetic and persistent support from Boris as those 'masters of the universe'. As Simon Jenkins, a journalist at the *Standard*, argues, Johnson's 'defense of bankers' greed is Bullingdon morality, pure and simple.'[5]

---

3 *The Times*, 4 March 2009, p. 3.
4 *The Times*, 21 March 2009, p. 4.
5 Purnell, pp. 400–1.

70. BORIS WAS RE-ELECTED MAYOR OF LONDON IN 2012

In the final weeks before the 2010 General Election, Tory leader David Cameron, who had been 'keen to associate himself with London's Conservative Administration' in the run-up to the vote, told the BBC that he was sure Johnson would seek re-election as Mayor of London. This prompted a rebuke from a mayoral spokesman, 'It is not a decision for David, it is a decision for Boris whether he stands again.' However, he went on to concede that Johnson 'will almost certainly stand'.[1]

A few months later there were claims, denied by Johnson, that he had threatened not to stand again if the new Conservative government carried through planned funding cuts to key transportation projects. Such cuts, it was thought, would undermine Johnson's re-election prospects.[2] Two weeks later, however, Boris announced that he would seek a second term as mayor.[3]

If Johnson sought to create a bit of suspense about his plans, his main rival did the opposite. Almost a year after he lost the 2008 London mayoral election, Ken Livingstone indicated that he would seek to return to his old job in 2012, running as an independent if not selected as the Labour candidate.[4] It did not come to that, for in late 2010 Livingstone beat former MP Oona King to claim the Labour nomination. In response to Livingstone's pledge to run on Johnson's broken promises and cuts to services, the deputy mayor expressed surprise at Labour's decision to 'exhume' the man sometimes known as Red Ken.[5]

---

1 'I expect Boris Johnson to stand for a second term as London mayor,' says David Cameron,' by Hélène Mulholland, 14 April 2010, theguardian.com.

2 'Mayor Johnson denies threat not to run again,' by Eleanor Harding, 30 August 2010, independent.co.uk.

3 'Boris Johnson to stand for re-election in 2012,' 10 September 2010, bbc. com.

4 'Livingstone seeks return as mayor,' 19 March 2009, news.bbc co.uk.

5 'Ken Livingstone wins Labour nomination for London mayor,' 24 September 2010, bbc.com.

By this point Cameron's enthusiasm for Johnson's re-election was even greater. Success would not only provide a boost to the Prime Minister's party but would probably pre-empt until at least 2016 a challenge to his leadership by the country's most popular Tory politician. 'And so to the question, "How do you solve a problem like Boris?" unlike previous party leaders, the Prime Minister has, it seems, found the perfect answer. It's conceivable, even probable, that Cameron wants a Boris victory in 2012 more than the man himself.'[6]

One important issue in the election was taxes. Livingstone, who previously had denounced those who avoided taxes, was criticised for hypocrisy when it became known that he was under investigation for claiming earnings at the corporate rate (of 20p) rather than personal income tax rate of 50p, saving £50,000 in the process.[7] A few weeks later, on a radio programme, Livingstone accused Johnson of also channelling earnings into a private company to avoid income tax. Afterwards, in the lift, Boris 'squared up to' Livingstone, shouting "You're a f***ing liar! You're a f***ing liar! You're a f***ing liar!"[8]

As expected, however, the biggest issue in the campaign was transport. Livingstone promised to cut public transport fares by 7 per cent, although his ability to finance this appeared dubious.[9] And even after Chancellor George Osborne provided funds that allowed Johnson to reduce a planned fare increase, polls showed that Ken's promise was a vote winner, at least partly because Boris was not trusted on public transport. 'He rarely travels on public transport and so

---

6 Purnell, pp. 421–2.

7 'Inquiry as Ken Livingstone saves thousands in tax bill,' by Andrew Gilligan, 17 March 2012, telegraph.co.uk.

8 'Swear waves: Bojo's sweaty rant at "liar" Ken at radio station,' by Jason Beattie, 3 April 2012, mirror.co.uk.

9 'Can London afford Ken Livingstone's plan to cut fares?' by Polly Curtis, 11 April 2012, theguardian.com.

perhaps fails to appreciate widespread anger and frustration about overcrowded and late trains, buses and Tubes.'[10]

When the votes were counted, however, Boris emerged triumphant again, though his 3 per cent margin was tighter than anticipated. Yet his victory was notable because Conservatives suffered heavy losses in other local elections, which saw Labour gain control of 32 councils around the country.[11]

10 Purnell, pp. 440–1.
11 'London mayor: Boris Johnson wins second term by tight margin,' 5 May 2012, bbc.com.

71. BORIS WAS CRITICISED FOR TIES TO JENNIFER ARCURI

In September 2019 the *Sunday Times* published allegations that while mayor of London, Boris Johnson failed to declare his relationship with Jennifer Arcuri, a young American businesswoman living in the capital. She reported accompanied him on three foreign trade missions 'despite being ineligible for any of them'. One of her companies received at least £11,500 in funding from a promotional body overseen by Johnson; a second got £100,000 from the culture department. The mayor also spoke at several meetings she organised and was reported to have frequently visited her flat during lunch breaks for what she later characterised as 'technology lessons'. When Boris, by now Prime Minister, was asked to clarify his relationship with Arcuri in light of the *Times* article, he refused to answer six times before saying only, 'Everything was done with complete propriety and in the normal way.'[1]

Following the allegations, the Greater London Authority ethics watchdog wrote to the Independent Office for Police Conduct so that the latter could 'assess whether or not it is necessary to investigate the former mayor of London for the criminal offence of misconduct in public office.' The IOPC was chosen because, in addition to being mayor, Johnson was chairman of the Metropolitan Police Authority. Separately, a junior minister announced a government review of the £100,000 award to Arcuri's company in early 2019.[2]

The Government Internal Audit Agency later ruled that the Department for Digital, Culture, Media & Sport's £100,000 award to Arcuri's firm was 'appropriate'.[3] Around the same time, the IOPC opted to delay its announcement about whether

1 'The Arcuri affair,' *The Economist* (US edition), 28 September 2019, p. 53.
2 'Boris Johnson referred to police watchdog over US businesswoman links,' 27 September 2019, bbc.com.
3 'Boris Johnson's friend Jennifer Arcuri is CLEARED over the £100,000 grant her tech firm received to help train cyber experts,' by Richard Spillett and Martin Robinson, 31 October 2019, dailymail.co.uk.

to investigate the Prime Minister until after General Election scheduled for 12 December. 'The decision prompted fury from Westminster politicians and London assembly members who said that it appeared that a ruling had been "suppressed" in order to protect Johnson from potentially damaging headlines at a crucial stage of the election campaign.' The IOPC justified its decision on the basis of 'purdah', the pre-election period in which civil servants are prohibited from making announcements seen as advantageous to any candidate or party. Critics countered that since an announcement that the IOPC would not investigate Johnson clearly would not violate purdah, then a contrary decision should not either.[4]

It subsequently was reported that Arcuri had confided in four friends that she and Johnson had been having a sexual affair that began while he was seeking a second term as mayor of London in 2012.[5] In November 2019 she gave an interview to ITV News in which she accused Johnson of casting her aside 'like I am some gremlin'. She claimed not to understand why Boris had 'blocked me and ignored me as if I was some fleeting one-night stand or some girl that you picked up at a bar because I wasn't – and you know that.'[6]

---

4 'Fury as decision on police watchdog inquiry into PM is shelved until after election,' by Mark Townsend, 9 November 2019, theguardian.com.

5 'U.S. Businesswoman Admitted Affair with Boris Johnson, U.K. Report Says,' by Benjamin Mueller, 29 September 2019, nytimes.com.

6 *The New York Times*, 18 November 2019, p. A6.

72. BORIS HIJACKED THE OLYMPICS

Although the 2012 Olympics were awarded to London on the watch of Mayor Ken Livingston, his successor, Boris Johnson quickly made them his own.

On the day that Team GB won its first gold medal, Boris managed to steal the limelight, at least somewhat, by getting stuck on a zip wire 20 feet in the air, wearing a safety helmet and holding a union flag in each hand. 'As onlookers snapped photos on their mobile phones, he tried humorous small talk before calling out in mock despair: "Get me a ladder!"' The previous day, in a surprise appearance at the beach volleyball, Boris 'started his own brand of the Mexican wave', prompting many of the 15,000 spectators to get to their feet. Johnson's antics made Eduardo Paes, Mayor of Rio, whose city would host the 2016 Olympic Games, somewhat apprehensive. Not only would Boris be a tough act to follow but Paes worried that his London counterpart might 'do something crazy when he hands over the flag'. Boris's response probably was not all that comforting. 'I want to reassure my friend Eduardo that there is no chance of me hanging onto the flag at the closing ceremony,' joked Johnson, before adding mischievously 'As protocol demands I will be handing it over to Eduardo – probably.'[1]

Johnson also put on a 'show-stealing performance' at the Olympics closing parade, though not in the manner Paes may have feared. Thanking British athletes, Boris elicited 'massive cheers and riotous laughter' saying, 'You routed the doubters and you scattered the gloomsters and for the first time in living memory you caused Tube train passengers to break into spontaneous conversations with their neighbours about subjects other than their trod-upon toes.' He continued, 'speaking as a spectator, you produced such paroxysms of tears and joy on the sofas of Britain that

1 'Boris Johnson gets stuck on a zip-wire celebrating Olympic gold,' by Hélène Mulholland, 1 August 2012, theguardian.com.

you probably not only inspired a generation but helped create one as well.'[2]

Despite his memorable moments in the Olympics, Johnson's role should not be exaggerated. There were signs of this seven years later, as contenders jockeyed to succeed Theresa May as Tory leader and Prime Minister. Some of Johnson's supporters claimed that Boris had 'delivered the Olympics'. In fact, he had played no role in the effort to win the games for London and very little in the provision of the infrastructure needed to host it. And the two major Olympic-related decisions he did make were not successful. He allowed Tory donor Lakshmi Mittal to sponsor the construction near Olympic Park of the Orbit statue, a structure 'entirely incongruous to its surroundings' and serving 'no function whatsoever, either during the Olympics or after', other than as an advert for Mittal's company. Johnson also was responsible for the 'terrible' deal with the owners of West Ham United Football Club, also Tory donors, to spend hundreds of millions of pounds trying to make the Olympic Stadium suitable for football. 'The consensus of opinion is that it is not suitable for football. And the rent paid by West Ham, spread over a hundred years, will still end up significantly less than the taxpayer has paid to convert it to keep them happy.'[3]

2 '"You probably not only inspired a generation but helped create one as well": Boris steals show with Olympic parade speech,' 10 September 2012, mirror.co.uk.

3 'Boris Johnson may have been London's cheerleader in 2012 but he did not 'deliver the Olympics'. Far from it,' by Tom Peck, 21 June 2019, independent.co.uk.

73. BORIS IRKED IRISH AND MALAYSIANS

In February 2012 Jemima Khan interviewed London Mayor Boris Johnson in *The New Statesman*. Asked what made him angry, Johnson responded, 'lefty crap ... like spending £20,000 on a dinner at the Dorchester [hotel] for Sinn Fein.' This reference to the annual St Patrick's Day Gala Dinner did not go down well with Irishmen in the capital and beyond. Shelagh O'Connor, a leader of London's Irish community, called Johnson's comments extremely disrespectful and demanded an apology. Christine Quigley, a Dublin native running as a Labour candidate for the London Assembly, said, 'Boris's lazy and stupid remark is utterly factually wrong.' The gala was self-financing, so it did not cost taxpayers anything. On the contrary, funds raised through the sale of tickets and sponsorships not only covered the cost of the dinner but also helped pay for the city's St Patrick's Day parade and a donation to a charity for London's Irish community. And invited guests ranged across the political spectrum. Johnson's comment was all the more curious because, while Ken Livingstone, his predecessor as Mayor, had backed the gala dinners, Boris had ended them when he took over.[1]

A month later, 'and struggling to get ahead in the polls', Johnson apologised, sort of. He told *The Irish Independent*, 'I am profoundly sorry if I have offended any Irish person,' adding that he had been trying to make 'a point about cost cutting'. He also wrote a letter to the Irish Cultural Centre in Hammersmith explaining that it was 'deeply upsetting' that his comments had been exploited to suggest that he had anti-Irish feelings. He went on to assert that while party members Martin McGuinness and Pat Doherty had been guests of honour at the 2008 gala, 'these were not dinners for Sinn Fein and, of course, I make absolutely no assumptions about the political

---

1 'Boris Johnson calls London St Patrick's Day event "Lefty Sinn Fein crap",' 11 February 2012, belfasttelegraph.co.uk.

allegiances of those who attended the dinners.' His apology for the 'unintended offence that I may have given' seems disingenuous since the offence presumably was intended.[2]

The following year, another off-the-cuff remark drew a similar reaction. At the opening of the World Islamic Economic Forum in London, Malaysian Prime Minister Najib Razak indicated that women comprised 68 per cent of the Muslim country's university intake for the previous year. Johnson interjected that females went to university because they had to 'find men to marry'. Although Johnson's comment clearly was intended as a joke, and did elicit some laughter, it also drew forth groans, especially, according to a member of the audience, 'from professional, hijab-wearing ladies'. The Mayor's official Twitter subsequently was 'bombarded' with posts from female graduates, some of whom sarcastically requested dating advice after somehow managing to finish their degrees 'with a first but no husband'.[3]

2 'Boris Johnson apologises to London Irish community,' by Samira Shackle, 13 March 2012, newstatesman.com.
3 'Boris Johnson criticised for suggesting women go to university to find husband,' by Alexandra Topping, 8 July 2013, theguardian.com.

74. BORIS CLAIMED CARS DROVE
FEMALE SUFFRAGE

In October 2013 Sir Drummond Bone, Master of the University of Oxford's Balliol College, interviewed London Mayor Boris Johnson, a fellow automobile enthusiast. Johnson argued that cars were vehicles of liberation. Specifically, he claimed that women's suffrage in Britain 'probably wouldn't have happened' had it not been for the motor car. That female enfranchisement did come to pass was 'basically because men realised that women were at the wheel of a machine that could run them down, and in the 1920s there was no argument, that was it.' When Sir Drummond noted that this was not a claim he had heard before, Boris asserted that in the 1890s reactionaries had seen bicycles as connected to the growing push for women's suffrage. As a result, they would hang bicycles from trees to indicate their displeasure that women were able to use these liberating pieces of technology. And when the combustion engine allowed women to travel at great speeds and to 'be in a position of command' of the machine, 'the gig was up for male domination, and quite right too.'[1]

The claim that the development of particular modes of transportation was decisive in the political emancipation of British women is, to put it mildly, unusual. Under escalating pressure from activists, Parliament supported female suffrage well before ownership of automobiles became widespread. In both 1910 and 1911 Bills providing for the enfranchisement of some women passed their second reading, only to be abandoned by the government. Women likely would have won the vote before 1918 had not the Great War intervened.[2] Automobile ownership did not become really widespread until the 1930s, spurred by deregulation and falling prices.[3]

---

1 'Boris Johnson interviewed by Sir Drummond Bone,' 22 October 2013, voicesfromoxford.org.

2 Rosen, Andrew, *Rise up, Women: The Militant Campaign of the Women's Social and Political Union, 1903-1914*, (London: Routledge & Kegan Paul, 1974), pp. 137, 160–2. Marr, Andrew, *The Making of Modern Britain*, (London: Pan, 2009), p. 178.

3 'How the thirties saw Britain fall in love with the car... and become a nation of road hogs,' by Juliet Gardiner, 1 February 2010, dailymail.co.uk.

75. BORIS CALLS LONDON ASSEMBLY, LABOUR MPS, 'INVERTEBRATE JELLIES'

In early 2013, Mayor Johnson arrived at the London Assembly ready to discuss his proposed budget. The meeting was expected to be both contentious and extensive because he was calling for a 7p-per-week cut in council tax that was projected to result in the closure of a dozen fire stations. Unfortunately, his deputy Baroness Borwick was stuck on a Tube train. This meant that his opponents had the two-thirds majority necessary to amend the budget. When it sought to do so, instead of questioning the mayor, he denounced his opponents as 'great supine protoplasmic invertebrate jellies'. He also sought to provoke jeers from firefighters in the public galleries. The Assembly asked him to leave, but his delaying tactics worked: Borwick at last arrived, allowing his budget to pass unchanged.[1]

Boris apparently was so pleased with the insult, and the attention it garnered, that he recycled it a few years later. In October 2017, Johnson, now Foreign Secretary, was asked in the Commons to reconcile previous assertions that if the EU asked for money for Brexit they could 'go whistle' with subsequent claims that the British were 'law-abiding bill-paying people' who would 'meet our obligations as we see them'. Johnson responded by denying that his statements had been faithfully represented. Rather, he implied that all he had done was to refuse to pay €100 billion to secure a divorce from the EU, a sum that was 'eye-watering and far too high'. He continued that Labour MPs, 'the supine, protoplasmic invertebrate jellies', would 'readily fork out' that much money if given a chance.[2]

---

1 'Boris Johnson calls London Assembly members "protoplasmic invertebrate jellies",' by John Higginson, 25 February 2013, metro.co.uk.
2 'Topical Questions,' vol. 629, 17 October 2017, hansard.parliament.uk.

76. BORIS TRADED JIBES WITH NICK CLEGG

After the 2010 General Election the Tories formed a coalition with the Liberal Democrats, whose leader, Nick Clegg, Boris had earlier described as a 'cut-price edition of David Cameron hastily knocked off by a Shanghai sweatshop to satisfy unexpected market demand'.[1]

Although Johnson praised Clegg for sacrificing his 'political life' to form a government despite 'protracted political humiliation', his tone changed markedly before the 2013 local elections. Now, according to Johnson, Clegg was a 'wobbling jelly of indecision and vacillation' whose 'single contribution to politics has been to do a U-turn on tuition fees and then make a song about it.'[2]

Several months later Johnson argued that more should be done to help the nation's brightest members. More broadly, he asserted, any discussion of equality should take into account variation in IQ levels. 'The harder you shake the pack, the easier it will be for some cornflakes to get to the top.' Speaking on his weekly radio programme soon thereafter, Clegg accused Johnson of 'careless elitism' for asserting that some people were not clever enough to succeed in life. Not only was it 'fairly unpleasant' to speak about people 'as if they were a breed of dogs' but Johnson's 'deterministic' view of IQ was 'complete anathema to everything' Clegg had stood for in politics.[3]

Johnson fired back by calling Clegg Cameron's 'lapdog', who 'has been converted by taxidermy' into a protective shield, much like Valerian, the only Roman Emperor to become a prisoner of war, who 'was skinned and hung on the wall'. So far as Clegg, 'a very, very decorative part of the constitution, fulfils any function it is to stop sensible policies being promulgated by this government.' Johnson concluded 'the sooner we are shot of the great yellow albatross of the Liberal Democrats in my view

---

1 Purnell, p. 404.
2 'Boris: Clegg is a "wobbling jelly of indecision and vacillation",' 20 February 2013, londonlovesbusiness.com.
3 'Nick Clegg accuses Boris Johnson of "careless elitism",' 28 November 2013, bbc.com.

the better.'[4] Johnson later described Clegg as a condom, saying the deputy Prime Minister was a 'lapdog-cum-prophylactic protection device for all the difficult things that David Cameron has to do that cheese off the rest of the ... you know what I mean.' Put another way, Clegg was 'a lapdog who's been skinned and turned into a shield to protect' the party leader from Tory rank-and-file anger at Government policies such as support for same sex marriage.[5]

Clegg replied, 'I think most Londoners listening to this would expect Boris Johnson to focus on the day job of sorting out our transport system, our housing crisis in London, rather than ever more exotic ways of describing his political opponents.'[6]

Clegg continued to fire back even after he had left the Government. Speaking weeks before the referendum on Britain's relationship with the EU, Clegg said that Johnson was 'acting like Donald Trump with a thesaurus'. He went on to accuse Johnson and other prominent politicians supporting the Leave campaign 'of using every trick in the book to try and distract and distort their way to history'. He also said that Johnson and fellow Leave champion Michael Gove 'are probably the only people who think their job prospects might actually improve if we leave the EU.'[7]

Several months later, Clegg called Johnson, by now Foreign Secretary, a 'mop-haired buffoon' who was embarrassing Britain. Specifically, he accused Boris of 'two-faced posturing', by 'claiming 80 million Turks could turn up at Dover if we were to remain in the EU and then without the slightest smidgen of embarrassment fly off to Ankara and say to the Turks "Welcome to the EU!"'[8]

4 'Boris Johnson attacks "lapdog" Nick Clegg for blocking "sensible policies",' by Nicholas Watt, 17 December 2013, theguardian.com.

5 'Nick Clegg is Boris Johnson's condom, Boris Johnson says,' by Matthew Holehouse, 7 January 2014, telegraph.co.uk.

6 'Nick Clegg responds to Boris Johnson's condom jibe: "Focus on the day job",' by Kashmir Gander, 9 January 2014, independent.co.uk.

7 'Boris Johnson is like Donald Trump with a thesaurus, says Nick Clegg,' by David Singleton, 3 June 2016, totalpolitics.com.

8 'Nick Clegg tells us how "mop-haired buffoon" Boris Johnson is embarrassing Britain,' by Adam Payne, 14 December 2016, businessinsider.com.

77. BORIS WROTE *THE CHURCHILL FACTOR*

The London Mayor's 2014 biography of Winston Churchill is at pains to emphasise the similarities between the author and his political hero. In the words of one review, 'Here is a maverick Tory politician, endowed in equal measure with fierce ambition, immense self-confidence and wide-ranging intellectual inquisitiveness; a man endowed with many obvious advantages in the great race of life, not only through innate aptitude but also through social privilege in his upbringing; a public figure with a populist touch that give him brand-name recognition with the electorate. Everyone knows "Boris", just as everyone once knew "Winston".' According to Johnson, Churchill, who started out as a Tory and then jumped to the Liberals for two decades before returning to the Conservative fold, 'wasn't what people thought of as a man of principle: he was a glory-chasing, goal-mouth-hanging opportunist'. But such sins, as well as Churchill's 'many epic cock-ups' can be forgiven, in Johnson's view, because the great man 'dared to try to change the entire shape of history'.[1]

But while the two politicians obviously share some important features – from a penchant for witticisms to the ability to overcome career setbacks that would have been the end of most men – it is their differences that seem most salient today, half a dozen years after the biography was published. For example, Johnson 'wonders out loud if Churchill had played away, while praising the sturdiness of his 56-year marriage to Clemmie.'[2] If he did cheat on his wife, Churchill at least had the decency to do so far more discretely than Johnson, who repeatedly publicly embarrassed Marina with his philandering. Similarly, while finances motivated both men to write extensively while in public office, the quality of their output seems rather divergent, to put it mildly. Churchill was awarded the 1953 Nobel

---

1 '"The Churchill Factor" by Boris Johnson,' by Peter Clarke, 24 October 2014, ft.com.

2 '"The Churchill Factor" review—Boris Johnson's flawed but fascinating take on his hero,' by John Kampfner, 3 November 2014, theguardian.com.

Prize in Literature for 'mastery of historical and biographical description as well as for brilliant oratory in defending exalted human values'.[3] His six-volume memoir of the Second World War remains indispensable to any who wishes to understand that conflict. Johnson's articles, books and speeches, by contrast, have occasionally garnered fleeting critical acclaim but seem unlikely to be remembered for long.

However, the most important reason that Boris is no Winston concerns political expediency. Churchill is widely considered Britain's best-ever Prime Minister in spite of rather than because of his opportunism. It was because, when the chips were down, he acted on conviction, not political expediency, arguing against the popular belief that Hitler could be appeased. Churchill's denunciation of the 1938 Munich Accord created such hostility in his Epping constituency that he faced a very real threat of being deselected by the local Conservative Association.[4] By telling the truth about the Nazis, and supporting rearmament at a time when this was seen to promote war, Churchill effectively made himself a political pariah, only to be vindicated by events.

Johnson has largely done the opposite. Churchill saved Britain from invasion by repeatedly uttering uncomfortable truths about a foreign menace. Johnson repeatedly lied or exaggerated the threat posed by the EU, gaining power and influence in the process. Instead of saving Britain, Johnson has recklessly and mendaciously imperilled it.

It is for this reason that he has been deemed the worst Prime Minister in living memory.[5]

3 'The Nobel Prize in Literature 1953,' nobelprize.org.
4 Jenkins, Roy, *Churchill*, (London: Pan Macmillan, 2001), pp. 531–4.
5 'The Reckoning,' *The Economist* (US edition), 28 September 2019, p. 12.

78. BORIS'S VIEWS OF DONALD TRUMP EVOLVED

In late 2015 US Republican presidential candidate Donald Trump called for a 'complete shutdown' of Muslim immigration to the US. He later asserted that large areas of London and Paris were 'no go' areas for police because of the large Muslim communities there. In response, London Mayor Boris Johnson said that Trump's comments about the city betray 'a quite stupefying ignorance that makes him frankly unfit to hold the office of President of the United States.' Although Johnson rejected calls to ban Trump from entering the UK, the mayor was not exactly ready to roll out the red carpet. 'I would invite him to come and see the whole of London and take him round the city, except I wouldn't want to expose any Londoners to any unnecessary risk of meeting Donald Trump.'[1]

Johnson further stated that 'Donald Trump's ill-informed comments are complete and utter nonsense.' Boris continued that crime had been falling in London, as it had in New York, and the only reason he would not go to some parts of the latter city 'is the real risk of meeting Donald Trump'.[2] However, a few months later Johnson did visit New York City, where he claimed to have been mistaken for Trump, an experience he characterised as 'one of the worst moments'. He also told an interviewer that he was 'genuinely worried' that Trump could become president.[3]

By late 2016, following his successful efforts to persuade his countrymen to vote to leave the EU, Johnson had become Foreign Secretary. His tune on Trump, who recently had been elected US President, had now changed considerably, with Boris saying he was 'looking forward' to working with the man he

1 'Boris Johnson says Donald Trump "betrays a stupefying ignorance that makes him unfit to be US President",' by Matt Dathan, 9 December 2015, independent.co.uk.

2 'Boris Johnson: "The only reason I would not visit some parts of New York is the real risk of meeting Donald Trump",' by Helena Horton, 8 December 2015, telegraph.co.uk.

3 'Boris Johnson: "I was mistaken for Donald Trump",' by Kate McCann, 21 March 2016, telegraph.co.uk.

previously had disparaged. By way of apparent justification for the U-turn, Johnson's spokesman asserted that many politicians previously had made comments about Trump but now the task at hand was 'to get on with the job'.[4]

A few days later Johnson implored his 'beloved European friends and colleagues' to snap out of the 'general doom and gloom' and 'collective whinge-o-rama' resulting from the US election. Trump, Boris averred, was a 'deal maker' who 'wants to do a free trade deal with the UK', something that not only would help bilateral relations but would be 'of great importance for stability and prosperity in the world'.[5]

Shortly before Trump's inauguration, Johnson went to the US to meet with senior advisors to the President-elect. Boris praised the incoming administration's 'very exciting agenda of change' and claimed that the UK would be 'first in line' for a post-Brexit trade deal with the US.[6]

By mid-2018, Johnson was recorded as telling a closed-door meeting that he was 'increasingly admiring of Donald Trump'. According to Johnson, if Trump did Brexit, 'He'd go in bloody hard… There'd be all sorts of breakdowns, all sorts of chaos. Everyone would think he'd gone mad. But actually, you might get somewhere. It's a very, very good thought.'[7]

But when a NATO summit was held in Britain in late 2019, Johnson, by now Prime Minister, was reported to be doing 'everything possible' to avoid meeting Trump, lest the president's substantial unpopularity undermine Tory prospects in the upcoming general election.[8]

---

4 'Boris Johnson carries out screeching U-turn on Donald Trump,' by Rob Merrick, 9 November 2016, independent.co.uk.

5 'Boris Johnson calls for end to 'whinge-o-rama' over Donald Trump,' by Peter Walker and Matthew Weaver, 11 November 2016, theguardian.com.

6 'Boris Johnson has completely changed how he talks about Donald Trump,' by Benjamin Kentish, 10 January 2017, independent.co.uk.

7 'Boris Johnson offers three reasons why he admires Trump, whom he once called "out of his mind",' by Siobhán O'Grady, 26 June 2018, washingtonpost.com.

8 'Boris Johnson is doing everything possible to avoid Trump,' by Henry Mance, 3 December 2019, ft.com.

79. BORIS COULD HAVE BEEN PRESIDENT OF THE UNITED STATES

On 19 June 1999, Boris Johnson fulfilled the second of three Constitutional requirements to become President of the United States. He had become a 'natural born citizen' of the US by virtue of his birth in New York City in 1964. Now, having attained his 35th birthday, he met a second criterion. Johnson also was some way toward overcoming the final hurdle – 14 years' residence in the US – having spent about a third of that period living in Connecticut and Washington, D.C., during his childhood. After a successful stint as *The Daily Telegraph*'s correspondent in Brussels, he presumably could have finagled a posting to America to complete his eligibility. For someone who, at a very early age, had expressed a desire to become 'world king' the US Presidency might have seemed the best available alternative.

However, in early 2015 Johnson announced he was giving up his US citizenship and, in the words Tim Shipman, political editor at *The Times*, 'at last putting a limit on his ambition'. Put another way, by making clear where his loyalties lay, Johnson was hoping to pave the way to succeed David Cameron as Prime Minister.[1] There might have been financial motivations as well. Uncle Sam expects his citizens to pay US taxes, no matter where they live. American tax authorities recently had indicated that Johnson owed them as a result of his capital gain from the sale of North London house. After describing the tax bill as 'absolutely outrageous,' Johnson eventually agreed to pay it.[2] Ceding his US citizenship would obviate such problems in the future.

Still, that is certainly a loss for the US, and maybe for the UK as well. There are no formal requirements to become British PM.

---

1 'Crikey! Boris gives up White House to bid for No 10,' Tim Shipman, 15 February 2015, thetimes.co.uk.
2 'London Mayor Boris Johnson agrees to pay US tax bill,' 22 January 2015, BBC.com.

Citizenship, while not strictly necessary, presumably would be helpful. Obtaining a 'Tier 1 investor' visa by, say, buying a golf resort in Scotland, could facilitate this. Given a choice between strange-haired, overweight, adulterous, egotistical, indolent, veracity-challenged hate mongers, surely US voters would opt for Boris Johnson over Donald Trump. For all his faults, the former clearly is more articulate (not a high bar), wittier, more erudite, and altogether more entertaining. Plus, Americans tend to go crazy for a British accent. By contrast British voters, and especially those who think things could not possibly get any worse, might (just possibly) lament that they have not been able to experience political leadership *a la* The Donald. And his New Yawk accent hardly would be an insuperable barrier to constant entertainment. After all, the English did once adopt a king (George I) who, as MP William Shippen pointed out in the Commons (shortly before his colleagues sent him to the Tower in 1717), was unacquainted with the country's language or constitution. So a trade could have been, if not mutually beneficial, at least potentially entertaining.

80. BORIS RETURNED TO PARLIAMENT IN 2015

In October 2011, not long before he was elected to a second term as Mayor of London, Johnson told an interviewer that a popular vote on Britain's relationship with the EU 'is not a bad idea', adding that its outcome would be 'far from a foregone conclusion'. Boris further stated that he would be 'very, very interested' in the outcome of 'an in-out referendum.' Johnson's position put him at odds with Tory leader David Cameron, who argued that leaving the EU would be economically detrimental to Britain and that most in the country shared that view. Evidently seeking to preclude speculation that his stance was taken in order to challenge Cameron for the premiership, Boris asserted, 'I don't think I will do another big job in politics' after leaving the mayor's office. He further stated that, despite media reports that he wanted to take over the party, there was 'not a snowball's chance in Hades' he would stand for Parliament if re-elected mayor of London.[1]

In early 2013, *GQ* named Johnson the most influential man in Britain, partly on the strength of a recent poll showing that 'the Tories would receive a massive six-point bounce should they appoint Boris party leader instead of Cameron, wiping out Labour's lead almost entirely.' The article acknowledged that 'Boris has always denied that he would run, but with a gleam in his eye that says otherwise.'[2]

A year later Mayor Johnson announced his intention to return to Parliament amid speculation that he sought to take over as Tory leader when Cameron stepped down. Specifically, Boris sought to become the Conservative candidate for Uxbridge and South Ruislip, a west London constituency whose retiring

---

1 'Boris Johnson says EU referendum would be a "good idea",' 5 October 2011, bbc.com.
2 'The 100 Most Influential Men in Britain 2013,' 7 February 2013, gq-magazine.co.uk.

MP Sir John Randall had garnered an 11,000-vote majority in the 2010 general election. If returned to Parliament in the 2015 General Election, Johnson indicated that he would serve out the remaining year of his mayoral term.[3]

Shortly thereafter, Johnson was selected to be the Conservative candidate for Uxbridge, defeating sixty-one others who had applied for the nomination for the Tory safe seat. Earlier Cameron indicated that he would be delighted to have Boris back in Parliament, stating that he wanted his 'star players on the pitch'.[4]

3 'Boris Johnson confirms Uxbridge as target seat,', 26 August 2014, bbc.com.
4 'Boris Johnson selected for Uxbridge and South Ruislip seat,' 12 September 2014, bbc.com.

81. BORIS BACKED BREXIT: CUI BONO?

In 2007 Conservative leader David Cameron issued a 'cast-iron guarantee' to hold a referendum on the Lisbon Treaty then being negotiated, only to anger many in his party by abandoning the pledge after other countries ratified the agreement.[1] Several years later, in a bid to rally his divided party ahead of the 2015 General Election, Cameron promised to renegotiate Britain's relationship with the European Union and allow the public to vote on whether to the UK should remain part of the organisation.[2] Soon after the election, an overwhelming majority (84 per cent) of MPs voted to hold a referendum, after Labour, which previously opposed such a move, opted to support it in the wake of its poor showing at the polls.[3] The date for the referendum eventually was established as 23 June 2016.

In the months before the referendum Johnson, who previously had evinced uncertainty about whether Britain should leave the bloc, began to campaign for that outcome with gusto. Cameron would later claim in his memoirs that Boris's choice of sides was determined by personal ambition rather than conviction: 'He risked an outcome he didn't believe in because it would help his political career.' However, Cameron undercuts that assertion by stating that Johnson had turned down the post of Minister of Defence in return for supporting the 'Remain' side, despite later predicting that Brexit would be crushed 'like the toad beneath the harrow'.[4] When Johnson announced that he was backing a vote to leave the EU, the pound suffered its worse fall since Cameron became Prime Minister, hitting a seven-year low.[5]

1 'David Cameron to shed "cast iron" pledge on Lisbon treaty,' by Nicholas Watt and Patrick Wintour, 3 November 2009, theguardian.com.
2 'U.K.'s Cameron Draws Fire Over Europe Plan,' by Cassell Bryan-Low, 23 January 2013, wsj.com.
3 'EU referendum: MPs support plan for say on Europe,' 9 June 2015, bbc.com.
4 *The New York Times*, 16 September 2019, p. A8.
5 'Pound hits a seven-year low after Boris Johnson's Brexit decision – as it happened,' by Graeme Wearden and Nick Fletcher, 22 February 2016, theguardian.com.

Even more of a concern than the apparent opportunism of Johnson's choice of sides were the tactics he and others in the Leave campaign employed. The campaign's 'battle bus' was emblazoned with the claim: 'We send the EU £350 million a week, let's fund our NHS instead.' This figure was highly disputed at the time, and when Johnson repeated the claim a year later, the head of the UK Statistics Authority accused him of a 'clear misuse of official statistics'.[6] In 2019 Johnson was summoned to appear at Westminster Magistrates' Court to answer charges of misconduct in public office for endorsing the 'lies' on the Brexit bus, but the ruling later was overturned by a judge who found that the charges could not be used in the context of political campaign statements.[7]

Equally misleading were Johnson's pre-referendum comments about Turkey. Although he repeatedly pointed out, correctly, that official policy was for Turkey to join the EU, he also co-signed a letter to the Prime Minister which claimed, falsely, that the pace of Turkey's accession negotiations were 'rapidly accelerating', implying millions of Turks soon would be able to travel to the UK unless the country divorced itself from the EU.[8]

After Barack Obama urged the UK to remain in the EU while on a visit to Britain, Johnson attributed the US President's remark to his 'part-Kenyan' background, implying that his accounted for an 'ancestral dislike of the British Empire'. Although UKIP leader Nigel Farage defended Boris's comments, politicians of all stripes, including many Conservatives, roundly condemned them.[9]

Finally, Boris implied that voting to leave actually would mean not having to do so, because the EU would respond to the threat of the UK's departure with such attractive concessions that it then would be in Britain's interest to remain.[10] So the country could both have its cake and eat it.

---

6 'Boris Johnson left isolated as row grows over £350m post-Brexit claim,' by Anushka Asthana, 17 September 2017, theguardian.com.

7 'Boris Johnson: Court quashes attempt to prosecute Prime Minister over Brexit bus "lies",' by Lizzie Dearden, 14 August 2019, independent.co.uk.

8 'Brexit: Did Boris Johnson talk Turkey during the referendum campaign?' by Chris Morris, 19 January 2019, bbc.com.

9 'Obama hits back at Boris Johnson's alleged smears,' 22 April 2016, bbc.com.

10 'No Boris, you can't have your Brexit cake and eat it too,' by Michael White, 22 February 2016, theguardian.com.

82. BORIS GETS TURKISH PRESIDENT'S GOAT

In March 2016 German comic Jan Boehmermann read on his late-night television programme an obscene poem about Turkish President Recep Tayyip Erdoğan, thereby intentionally violating a law prohibiting the insulting of foreign leaders. Erdoğan responded by filing a criminal complaint. This prompted a Hamburg court to prohibit Boehmermann from repeating obscene elements of the poem, particularly references to sex with goats and sheep. This decision provoked debate about German freedom of speech, including in the country's legislature, where an MP read the unexpurgated poem in the context of a proposal to abolish the law in question.[1]

In Britain, *The Spectator* responded with the 'President Erdoğan offensive poetry competition', the £1,000 prize for which was donated by a reader. Thousands entered, but Boris won even though he did not officially do so. Complaining in an interview about the court injunction, Johnson opined, 'If somebody wants to make a joke about the love that flowers between the Turkish president and a goat, he should be able to do so, in any European country, including Turkey.' Challenged by the interviewer to enter the contest, Boris composed the following off the cuff:

> There was a young fellow from Ankara
> Who was a terrific wankerer
> Til he sowed his wild oats
> With the help of a goat
> But he didn't even stop to thankera

The contest's judge, Douglas Murray, conceded that Johnson's was not the best poem he had received, and that 'wankerer'

---

1 'German court rules against comic Boehmermann over Erdogan poem,' 17 May 2016, bbc.com.

was not even a word. But he argued that the prize was 'entirely anti-meritocratic' and that it was 'a wonderful thing that a British political leader has shown that Britain will not bow before the putative caliph in Ankara.'[2]

2 'Boris Johnson wins 'most offensive Erdogan poem' competition,' by Jessica Elgot, 19 May 2016, theguardian.com.

83. BORIS WAS APPOINTED FOREIGN SECRETARY

When British voters chose to 'Leave' the EU, David Cameron, who had called the referendum and supported the 'Remain' campaign, found his position untenable as both Prime Minister and Tory leader. His resignation led to a scramble to replace him, with around a dozen MPs thought to be seriously considering a leadership bid. Johnson, a leading advocate of Brexit, was widely viewed as the favourite, both because he had the support of many of the roughly 130 Conservative MPs in the 'Leave' camp and because he had demonstrated considerable grassroots appeal over the course of the campaign.[1]

But in late June 2016, Michael Gove, hitherto one of Johnson's closest pro-Brexit allies, announced his own bid to become Prime Minister, having come, 'reluctantly, to the conclusion that Boris cannot provide the leadership or build the team for the task ahead'. This prompted enough MPs to shift their support from Johnson that he soon announced he was no longer a candidate to succeed Cameron. Dominic Raab, in explaining why he switched his support from Johnson to Gove, said 'Boris was cavalier with assurances he made,' presumably about who would get what posts in his administration. Another MP, Business Minister Anna Soubry, apologised for the chaos, revealing that she would back Home Secretary Theresa May because 'We've had enough of these boys messing about.' Lord Heseltine accused Johnson of having 'ripped the Tory party apart', creating 'the greatest constitutional crisis in peacetime in my life' by campaigning for Brexit but then refusing to try to implement it. Johnson was, according to Heseltine, 'like a General who marches his army to the sound of guns and the moment he sees the battleground he abandons it.'[2]

Boris Johnson in 100 Facts

---

1 'Boris Johnson favorite to replace David Cameron after Brexit,' by Rowena Mason, 24 June 2016, theguardian.com.
2 'Conservative MPs in uproar as Boris Johnson "rips party apart" by withdrawing from leadership contest after ambush from Michael Gove,' by Laura Hughes, 30 June 2016, telegraph.co.uk.

As a result of Gove's surprise move, 'the most spectacular political assassination in a generation', May became the clear favourite to take over the leadership of the Conservative Party.[3] Johnson soon endorsed another candidate for the leadership, Andrea Leadsom, who, unlike May, had backed the Leave campaign.[4] However, when Leadsom dropped out of the race a few days later, May became Britain's second female Prime Minister. She named Johnson Foreign Secretary in her new government.[5]

The appointment as Britain's top diplomat of a man not known for his tact provoked not a few eye rolls, both at home and abroad. *The Daily Mirror* reacted with a picture of the new Foreign Secretary on the cover, along with the words, 'dear world … sorry.' Former Swedish Prime Minister Carl Bildt tweeted that he 'wished it was a joke'. But while not without risks for May, the decision to make Johnson Foreign Secretary had political logic. The post was considerably weaker than it had been previously, with responsibility for negotiating the terms of Brexit outside its purview. The Foreign and Commonwealth Office is now primarily concerned with promoting British interests overseas, meaning that its leader needed to be more a salesman than a statesman. This was seen to make the job a good fit for Johnson, 'a man who easily makes up in charm what he lacks in gravitas.' And while giving Boris a senior cabinet position would mollify those in the party who supported Brexit, this particular post would require him to spend considerable time outside Britain, reducing his capacity to make trouble for May.[6]

3 'Boris Johnson's allies accuse Michael Gove of "systemic and calculated plot" to destroy his leadership hopes,' by Steven Swinford, Christopher Hope, and Peter Dominiczak, 30 June 2016, telegraph.co.uk.
4 'Boris Johnson endorses Andrea Leadsom in Tory leadership bid,' by Anushka Asthana and Rowena Mason, 4 July 2016, theguardian.com.
5 'Boris Johnson made Foreign Secretary by Theresa May,' 13 July 2016, bbc. com.
6 'Why Making Boris Johnson Britain's Foreign Secretary is a Smart Move,' by Dan Stewart, 14 July 2016, time.com.

84. BORIS WAS UNDIPLOMATIC AS FOREIGN SECRETARY (HOLD THE FRONT PAGE)

To the surprise of almost nobody, Johnson's tenure as Foreign Secretary was marked by repeated gaffes. Some suggested policy disagreements within the Government. For example, when in December 2016 Johnson asserted that Saudi Arabia had been 'playing proxy wars' in the Middle East, this provoked 'an almost unprecedented rift' with Prime Minister Theresa May, whose official spokesman indicated that the Foreign Secretary's comments were 'not the Government's position'.[1]

Other verbal blunders appear prompted by little more than carelessness. In late 2017 Johnson told a parliamentary committee that Nazanin Zaghari-Ratcliffe, a British-Iranian woman who had been sentenced by Iran to five year's imprisonment for attempting to overthrow the government, had been 'simply teaching people journalism'. This assertion was at odds with Mrs Zaghari-Ratcliffe's claim to have done nothing more than to take her daughter to meet her grandmother. For days later, she was summoned to court, where Johnson's comment was used as evidence to support accusations that she had engaged in 'propaganda against the regime', prompting fears that her sentence could be doubled.[2]

During an official visit to Myanmar in January 2017, Johnson began reciting 'The Road to Mandalay', a colonial-era poem by Rudyard Kipling. The 'visibly tense' UK ambassador to Myanmar felt compelled to intervene, telling the Foreign Secretary that his choice of verse was 'not appropriate'. The director of the Burma Campaign UK later said that it showed 'incredible insensitivity' for Johnson to recite such a poem at a time when resentment of British colonialism is tied to increased Buddhist nationalism in Myanmar.[3]

1 'Row over Saudi Arabia comments blows open rift between Theresa May and Boris Johnson,' by Peter Dominiczak, 9 December 2016, telegraph.co.uk.

2 'Fears for Nazanin Zaghari-Ratcliffe after Boris Johnson remark,' 6 November 2017, bbc.com.

3 'Boris Johnson caught on camera reciting Kipling in Myanmar Temple,' by Robert Booth, 29 September 2017, theguardian.com.

During the 2017 election campaign, Johnson promised to end Indian tariffs on British whisky during a visit to a Sikh temple in Bristol. This prompted a Sikh woman to complain that it was 'absolutely outrageous' for the Foreign Secretary to promote alcohol, the drinking of which is forbidden in Sikhism, in such a location. Boris responded, 'I am very sorry if you think alcohol is a bad thing. I understand your point of view,' but when asked if he would actually apologise, Johnson, whose mother-in-law is Sikh, replied 'I was making a very good point that I will continue to make.'[4]

At the 2017 Conservative Party Conference, Johnson spoke of the efforts of UK business people who were seeking to turn the Libyan coastal city of Sirte 'into the next Dubai', before joking 'the only thing they have to do is clear the dead bodies away.' Baroness Stroud, host of the event at which Johnson was speaking, hurriedly intervened to say 'next question' while he continued to speak, but the damage was done, with even members of his own party lambasting the Foreign Secretary's comments about the victims of Libya's civil war as 'crass, poorly judged and grossly insensitive'.[5]

When asked by Belgium's Ambassador to the EU about the concerns of corporate leaders about the consequences of Brexit at a Foreign Office reception celebrating the Queen's birthday in mid-2018, Boris replied, 'Fuck business.' Johnson went on to promise that he would fight Prime Minister Theresa May's 'soft' Brexit 'and win'. Asked about the Foreign Secretary's comments, another EU diplomat replied, 'I was shocked by how crude and crass he was, as if he did not care for the consequences and especially not the economic consequences of Brexit.'[6]

4 'Boris Johnson criticised by Sikh woman over whisky comment in Gurdwara,' 17 May 2017, bbc.com.
5 'Boris Johnson Libya "dead bodies" comment provokes anger,' 4 October 2017, bbc.com.
6 'EU diplomats reveal Boris Johnson said "f**k business" over Brexit fears,' 23 June 2018, thenational.scot.

85. BORIS RESIGNED AS FOREIGN SECRETARY IN JULY 2018

In early July 2018, Prime Minister Theresa May held a cabinet meeting at Chequers that produced a government white paper laying out the sort of relationship with the EU the UK sought to achieve through the Brexit negotiations. Senior EU officials had rejected key elements of the Chequers plan even before it was announced, so its eventual demise was not a surprise.[1] Less anticipated was that May's attempt to reconcile a divided cabinet at Chequers would instead provoke the resignations of David Davis, the Brexit Secretary, Steve Baker, his parliamentary under-secretary, and Foreign Secretary Boris Johnson, all of whom scorned the plan.

Johnson, who reportedly likened attempts to promote the plan to 'polishing a turd', seems to have felt compelled to resign only after Davis and Baker did so. Downing Street, in what might be interpreted as an indication that Boris would not be missed, announced that he was stepping down before Johnson had a chance to complete his resignation letter. Or it may have been an attempt to steal his thunder, for in that epistle Johnson derided May's scheme as 'a semi-Brexit' that would relegate Great Britain to 'the status of a colony' by leaving large segments of the economy 'locked in the EU system, but with no UK control over that system'. Breaking with convention, Johnson released his letter before Downing Street had a chance to reply.[2]

A week later in the Commons, Johnson accused May of 'dithering' over a strategy to leave the EU. He further asserted that it was 'not too late to save Brexit' but that any agreement that required the UK to follow EU trade, environment and social regulations risked consigning the country to 'economic vassalage'.

---

1 'All the times EU has said "no" to Theresa May's Chequers Brexit trade plan,' by Jon Stone, 21 September 2018, independent.co.uk.

2 'May's plan "sticks in the throat", says Boris Johnson as he resigns over Brexit,' by Heather Stewart, Pippa Crerar and Dan Sabagh, 9 July 2018, theguardian.com.

The speech was notable not only for the highly unusual absence of any jokes by Boris but also for the 'pretty savage attack' on May's policies. However, Johnson's allies were adamant that he was not seeking to emulate Sir Geoffrey Howe, whose 1990 resignation speech helped end Margaret Thatcher's premiership.[3]

If Johnson was angling to replace May, his performance as Foreign Secretary hardly seemed to have helped. His mission was to convince outsiders that Brexit would not mean Britain's withdrawal from world affairs. According to one analysis, 'few historians will conclude' that Boris managed to achieve this goal. Indeed, he resigned as he was supposed to be chairing a summit on the West Balkans that was meant to show the UK's enduring commitment to European security. Although many had hoped that Johnson's star power would increase Britain's international profile, his repeated gaffes and lack of substance soon led to disappointment. While the world waited for Britain to articulate policies regarding the rise of China and India, conflicts involving Syria and North Korea and sub-Saharan migration, Johnson focused on women's education and saving elephants, laudable issues but perhaps not sufficient to enhance Britain's international stature.[4]

Despite such shortcomings in a senior cabinet role, Johnson was soon reported to be in private conversations with Steve Bannon, former chief advisor to US President Donald Trump, who urged him to challenge May for the leadership of the Conservative Party.[5]

3 'Boris Johnson: It's not too late to save Brexit,' 18 July 2018, bbc.com.
4 'Boris Johnson: what did he achieve as Foreign Secretary?' by James Landale, 9 July 2018, bbc.com.
5 'Boris Johnson has been privately talking to Steve Bannon as they plot their next moves,' by J. Lester Feder, Mark Di Stefano and Alex Spence, 25 July 2018, buzzfeednews.com.

86. BORIS WAS FORCED TO APOLOGISE TO PARLIAMENT

Soon after resigning as Foreign Secretary, Johnson signed a contract to write a column for the *Daily Telegraph*. The Advisory Committee on Business Appointments, a public watchdog established in 1975 to try to prevent conflicts of interests by former senior Crown servants and Ministers, subsequently criticised Boris both for failing to seek its advice before signing the contract and for not observing the mandatory three-month waiting period before assuming the new position. Jon Trickett, Labour's Shadow Cabinet Office Minister, responded by lambasting Johnson for his 'utter contempt' for 'democracy and ridding politics of vested interests' and calling for a 'drastic overhaul' of ACOBA, a 'toothless body,' so that the country 'can put an end to politicians and the establishment working only for the interests of themselves'. The Commons' Public Administration and Constitutional Affairs Committee also called for significant reforms to the watchdog in order to improve public trust.[1]

Several months later, Johnson was forced to apologise to Parliament for failure to report his full earnings to the House, a highly embarrassing outcome for a man who was widely seen to be preparing to challenge Prime Minister Theresa May for the leadership of the Conservative Party. The Parliamentary Commissioner for Standards found that Johnson had failed to declare more than £50,000 in earnings. It further asserted that his failure to register his earnings within the required time period on nine separate occasions, 'suggested a lack of attention to the House's requirements, rather than an inadvertent error'. Boris later acknowledged that his delayed filings breached House rules, offering the Commons 'a full and unreserved apology'.[2]

1 'Boris Johnson broke ex-minister rules over *Telegraph* contract,' 9 August 2018, bbc.com.
2 'Boris Johnson ordered to apologise to Parliament for failing to declare earnings,' by Adam Bienkov, 6 December 2018, businessinsider.com.

87. BORIS WAS CRITICISED FOR SEX-ABUSE COMMENTS

On an early 2019 radio call-in programme Johnson characterised the £60 million being spent on non-recent child abuse investigations as 'spaffed up a wall'. He asserted that 'an awful lot of money and an awful lot of police time now goes into these historic offences and all this malarkey,' implying that it does little to protect the public today. Johnson's remarks came hours after an Australian court sentenced Cardinal George Pell to six years in prison for abusing two 13-year-old choirboys in 1996. They also follow the establishment of an investigation into multiple abuse scandals that came to light in the wake of similar revelations regarding entertainer Jimmy Savile. At the time of Johnson's remarks, the inquiry was in the middle of examining claims involving politicians. Shadow Minister for Policing Louise Haigh called Boris's comments insulting to abuse survivors, asking him 'Could you look the victims in the eye and tell them that investigating and bringing to justice those who abused them, as children, is a waste of money?' A Johnson ally responded that the man widely expected to soon become Conservative leader had no intention of apologising or clarifying his remarks, pointing out that spending on front line policing and addressing knife crime should be prioritised over historic cases in which the alleged perpetrator was dead.[1]

One abuse victim called Johnson's comments 'horrific'. The leader of a charity aimed at helping survivors of child sexual abuse in football described them as 'ignorant, dangerous, disgraceful and unbelievably distasteful'. The head of another charity characterised the remarks as 'insensitive and ill-informed', particularly given the vast sums Johnson wasted on vanity projects as mayor of London.[2]

---

1 'Boris Johnson under fire for remarks about child abuse inquiries,' by Dan Sabbagh, 13 March 2019, theguardian.com.
2 'Boris Johnson historical child sex abuse comments "horrific"', 13 March 2019, bbc.com.

88. BORIS PROVOKED 'OPEN CIVIL WAR' AMONG TORIES OVER BREXIT PLAN

Two months after resigning from Prime Minister Theresa May's cabinet over the so-called Chequers Plan for negotiating Brexit, Johnson fostered 'open civil war' in the Conservative Party with a piece in the *Mail on Sunday*. He argued that, to date, 'Brussels gets what Brussels wants' because of repeated concessions by May to the EU and its chief negotiator Michel Barnier. For Britain to agree to rules that it would have no say in making would be 'a humiliation. We look like a seven-stone weakling being comically bent out of shape by a 500lb gorilla.' More controversially still, Boris excoriated provisions for a 'backstop' that would prevent the re-establishment of a hard Irish border by keeping Northern Ireland part of the single market until a workaround could be devised. 'We have opened ourselves,' he asserted, 'to perpetual political blackmail. We have wrapped a suicide vest around the British constitution – and handed the detonator to Michel Barnier.' This claim elicited vehement denunciations from senior Tories. Sir Alan Duncan, Minister of State for Europe and the Americas, called Johnson's comment 'one of the most disgusting moments in modern British politics' and vowed that if it did not mark 'the political end of Boris Johnson' then he would make sure it came later. Alistair Burt, Parliamentary Under-Secretary of State for Foreign and Commonwealth Affairs, proclaimed himself 'stunned' by Johnson's comment, adding, 'There is no justification for such an outrageous, inappropriate and hurtful analogy.' One senior Conservative backbencher, Sarah Wollaston, indicated she likely would quit the party if Johnson became its leader because 'I don't think he's fit to lead the country.' Another, Dominic Grieve, who recently had made a similar pledge, called Johnson's phrasing 'entirely in character: crude but, for some, entertaining populist polemic'. Still others, 'a bit tired of the Boris show', suggested that Johnson might be more likely to oust May than replace her.[1]

---

1 'Tories in civil war after Boris Johnson Brexit "suicide vest" remarks,' by Peter Walker, 10 September 2018, theguardian.com.

However, Johnson allies sprung to his defence. Zac Goldsmith suggested that while there might be various motives behind Duncan's tweet, 'given its author, we can be certain "principles" aren't one of them.' Jacob Rees-Mogg, a senior Brexiteer, indicated that the row over Johnson's 'characteristically colourful catchphrase' should not obscure the reality that many in the party agree with his criticism of the Chequers plan. And Nadine Dorries implied that the backlash was due less to the nature of Boris's remarks than the fact that his opponents were 'terrified of his popular appeal... He delivered the Leave vote, Remainers and wannabe future PMs hate him.' Still others blamed May for the underlying problem, of which Johnson's comments were merely a symptom. By putting forth the Chequers proposals without previously seeking widespread input about them, May was seen not only as causing problems for her own leadership but also of risking a 'catastrophic split' in the Conservative Party.[2]

2 'Tories at war over Boris Johnson "suicide vest" jibe at May over her Chequers Brexit plan,' by Benjamin Kentish, 10 September 2018, independent.co.uk.

89. BORIS AND SECOND WIFE FILED FOR DIVORCE

After rejoining the Tories after two decades sitting on the Liberal benches, Winston Churchill memorably said 'Anyone can rat, but it takes a considerable amount of ingenuity to re-rat.'[1] As perhaps the most notorious love rat in British politics, Boris also displayed a certain ingenuity by engaging in repeated (and not very clandestine) affairs while remaining married to his second wife, Marina Wheeler. But in September 2018 Johnson's 25-year-period of having his cake and eating it came to an end as he and Marina announced plans to divorce. This came shortly after *The Sun* reported she was no longer was living or socialising with him for cheating on her yet again, allegedly ditching the police assigned to protect the Foreign Secretary to carry out trysts. However, few expected these developments to affect Johnson's prospects of becoming Conservative leader. As one Tory MP commented, 'It's all priced in because I don't think any of his buffoonery will surprise anyone.'[2]

Maybe, but around the same time, rumours, denied by Prime Minister Theresa May's office, were circulating in Westminster that a dossier of Johnson's infidelities had been provided to MPs. The 4,000-word document had been compiled for the 2016 Conservative leadership election by Nick Hargrave, then May's deputy head of policy, in the hopes that a litany of Johnson's transgressions would dissuade party members from voting for him. It was not used in 2016 because Johnson did not stand for the leadership after Michael Gove undercut his support. But in 2018, with Boris clearly angling for May's job amid rumours that an affair with former Tory spin doctor Carrie Symonds was responsible for his divorce, there was conjecture

---

1 Enright, Dominique, 'The Wicked Wit of Winston Churchill', (London: Michael O'Mara Books, 2001), p. 23.
2 'Boris Johnson and Marina Wheeler announce divorce,' by Peter Walker, 7 September 2018, theguardian.com.

that No. 10 was finally making use of its research in a desperate effort to thwart a popular challenger.[3]

If Boris expected his split with Wheeler to keep his love life out of the papers, he soon learned otherwise. In mid-2019 *The Guardian* reported that police had been called in the early morning hours to the house Johnson was sharing with Symonds 'after neighbours heard a loud altercation involving screaming, shouting and banging.' A neighbour, concerned about Symonds's welfare, recorded the row, in which the former Conservative Party head of press is heard telling the man widely expected to soon become Prime Minister to 'get off me' and 'get out of my flat.' Johnson is heard not only refusing to leave but telling Symonds to 'get off my fucking laptop' before there is a 'loud crashing noise'. Symonds then berates Boris for spilling red wine on the sofa, adding, 'You don't care for anything because you're spoilt.' The police took no action after speaking to the two and being assured both were safe and no offences had been committed.[4]

---

3 'Dossier of Boris Johnson's misdeeds circulated around Westminster,' by Adam Smith, 9 September 2018, metro.co.uk.
4 'Boris Johnson: police called to loud altercation at potential PM's home,' by Jim Waterson, 21 June 2019, theguardian.com.

90. BORIS BASHES BURKAS

In response to Dutch legislation prohibiting the wearing of clothing covering the face, such as ski masks, balaclavas and burkas, Boris took to the pages of *The Telegraph* in early August 2018 to denounce such a ban. But he also stated that he felt 'fully entitled' to ask women who came to his MP surgery wearing such items to remove them and believed educational authorities should be able to do the same should a student turn up 'looking like a bank robber'. He further opined that 'the burka is oppressive', and that 'it is absolutely ridiculous that people should go around looking like letter boxes.' Labour MPs denounced Johnson for stoking Islamophobia, with one Britain's most prominent Muslims, Baroness Warsi, accusing the former Foreign Secretary of practicing 'dog whistle' politics.[1]

As outrage over his remarks grew, Conservative Party chairman Brandon Lewis and Prime Minister Theresa May both made it clear that Johnson should apologise. His allies indicated that this would not happen, apparently because an apology would make him appear weak as he contends for the party leadership. So instead of acknowledging that his choice of words caused offence, Boris sought to turn the debate into whether burkas should be worn at all.[2]

Reaction to Johnson's comments, which came amid indications of an increase in Islamophobic violence and growing criticism of the Conservative Party for not addressing anti-Muslim prejudice within its ranks, continued to mount. Former Attorney General Dominic Grieve characterised Boris's behaviour as 'very embarrassing' and pledged 'without the slightest doubt' to quit the Tories should Johnson become leader, 'because I don't regard him as a fit and proper person to lead a political party.' Scottish Conservative leader Ruth Davidson called for Johnson to apologise for what she termed

---

1 'Boris Johnson faces criticism over burka "letter box" jibe,' 6 August 2018, bbc.com.
2 'Boris Johnson "won't apologise" for burka comments,' 7 August 2018, bbc. com.

his 'gratuitously offensive' remarks. Johnson's supporters dismissed the furore as politically motivated, arguing that other senior Conservatives had made similar comments without provoking such a reaction. Yet it seems the reaction was precisely the point, for 'as ever, being outspoken is at once appealing to Boris Johnson's supporters and distasteful to his detractors.'[3]

As the Conservative Party was inundated by complaints about Johnson's disparaging statements it decided an independent panel should investigate them. This body could then refer him to the Party's board for possible sanctions, including suspension and expulsion. The party's code of conduct requires its officials and elected representatives to 'lead by example to encourage and foster respect and tolerance' and refrain from using their position 'to bully, abuse, victimise, harass or unlawfully discriminate against others'.[4]

Four months later the panel absolved Johnson of any culpability for his remarks, finding that while his language might be considered 'provocative' he had been 'respectful and tolerant' and had been entitled to use 'satire' to make his point. A Boris ally later called on Lewis, the party chairman, to 'do the honourable thing' and apologise to Johnson 'with the same zeal he shamelessly used to smear his name during the summer.'[5]

As for the Dutch ban that set off the kerfuffle, it proved much ado about almost nothing as police and transport companies declined to enforce it.[6]

3 'Boris Johnson faces growing criticism over burka jibe,' 8 August 2018, bbc.com.

4 'Boris Johnson facing Tory investigation over burka comments,' 9 August 2018, bbc.com.

5 'Boris Johnson cleared by investigation into burka comments,' by Aubrey Allegretti, 21 December 2018, news.sky.com.

6 'Dutch "burqa ban" rendered largely unworkable on first day,' by Daniel Boffey, 1 August 2019, theguardian.com.

91. BORIS WAS BITTEN BY PRESS WATCHDOG OVER BREXIT CLAIM

Johnson's 7 January 2019 *Daily Telegraph* column was entitled, 'The British people won't be scared into backing a woeful Brexit deal nobody voted for.' He claimed that despite efforts by Remain supporters to exaggerate the dangers of a no-deal Brexit, this option was growing in popularity. Indeed, it 'is by some margin preferred by the British public.' This assertion prompted a complaint to the Independent Press Standards Organization. In defence of the article, *The Telegraph* argued that Boris was 'entitled to make sweeping generalisations based on his opinions' and that the piece 'was clearly comically polemical, and could not be reasonably read as a serious, empirical, in-depth analysis of hard factual matters.' Moreover, readers would understand that Johnson's claim 'was not invoking specific polling' because it did not indicate the dates on which opinion surveys had been conducted. Perhaps not surprisingly, the IPSO rejected the newspaper's contention that Boris basically could make up facts on whim. It ruled that he had breached the Editors' Code of Practice by failing to show sufficient diligence over the accuracy of his claims. Specifically, the press watchdog stated 'The reference to the polling was not material to the author's polemical argument. However, it was a significant inaccuracy, because it misrepresented polling information.' The *Telegraph* was ordered to print a correction to Johnson's article.[1]

The paper's online correction stated: 'In fact, no poll clearly showed that a no-deal Brexit was more popular than the other options.' Mitchell Stirling, the statistician who had filed the IPSO complaint, did so because he felt 'a potential Prime Minister shouldn't be able to make things up in a weekly column.'[2]

---

1 'Boris Johnson *Telegraph* column breached accuracy rules with claim of popular support for no-deal Brexit,' by Charlotte Tobitt, 12 April 2019, pressgazette.co.uk.
2 '*Telegraph* forced to correct false Brexit claim by Boris Johnson,' by Jim Waterson, 12 April 2019, theguardian.com.

92. BORIS BECOMES PRIME MINISTER

In late May 2019, after Parliament had thrice rejected deals she had negotiated with the EU, Theresa May announced that she would resign as Conservative leader. Ten candidates declared their intention to replace her. By rule, Tory MPs were to winnow the candidates down to two, with the party's members choosing the leader from between them. In the first round of voting, three candidates were eliminated. Boris received 114 votes, well ahead of his closest challengers, Jeremy Hunt (43) and Michael Gove (37).[1]

Evidently seeking to avoid a gaffe that might jeopardise his lead, Johnson then skipped the first televised debate among the candidates, eliciting criticism from his rivals. One of them, Dominic Raab, said 'If you can't take the heat of the TV studios what chance of taking the heat of the negotiating chamber in Brussels?' Channel 4, the debate's broadcaster, represented Boris with an empty podium.[2]

Johnson also pulled far ahead in the fund-raising contest, hoovering up more than £500,000 in political donations in a matter of weeks. Hunt, his closest rival, managed to rake in a bit more than £185,000 in the same period.[3]

In the end, Johnson and Hunt were the last two candidates standing, with Boris winning the lion's share of MP support as the best man to see off the challenge from Nigel Farage's insurgent Brexit Party. The 87.4 per cent of the Conservative Party's 159,320 members that voted in the leadership contest in July agreed, supporting Boris over Hunt by a two-to-one margin, 92,153 to 46,656.[4] He became only the second Prime Minister born outside the British Isles (after Andrew Bonar Law) and the first born in the US.[5]

1 'Boris Johnson tops first ballot in Tory leadership contest,' 13 June 2019, bbc.com.
2 'Say nothing, do nothing: Boris Johnson accused of ducking debates to avoid sabotaging leadership campaign,' 16 June 2019, sundaypost.com.
3 'Boris Johnson has received £500,000 in donations since May,' by Peter Walker, 17 July 2019, theguardian.com.
4 'Boris Johnson elected new Tory leader,' by Heather Stewart, 23 July 2019, theguardian.com.
5 'Boris Johnson becomes first US born Prime Minister of Britain,' 23 July 2019, theamerican.co.uk.

93. BORIS ASKS QUEEN TO PROROGUE PARLIAMENT

From his first days as Prime Minister, Boris made it clear that he was determined to take Britain out of EU by the end of October 2019, even if this meant departing without a transitional deal. But while MPs had rejected the Brexit agreements Theresa May had negotiated, they also had made it clear that they did not support a no-deal Brexit. Both those in Opposition and some moderate Conservative MPs were expected to support parliamentary measures that would prevent such an outcome. However, in late August, while MPs were on summer recess, Johnson asked the Queen to prorogue Parliament for five weeks. His justification was that the parliamentary session, already the longest in almost 400 years, needed to be brought to a close to allow him to bring forward 'a new bold and ambitious domestic legislative agenda'. But many suspected that the extended suspension of Parliament was intended to hinder the ability of opponents to prevent a no-deal Brexit, a motivation Boris and his allies disclaimed.[1]

The surprise move sparked 'Stop the Coup' protests in more than 30 cities and towns across the UK, and even in a few European capitals. A petition against the suspension of Parliament quickly received more than 1.5 million signatures. And former Tory Prime Minister Sir John Major indicated that he would back a legal challenge to his successor's action.[2]

Johnson's machinations also helped unite his opponents. Soon after MPs returned from recess, they voted to block a no-deal Brexit. Johnson then indicated that the party whip would be removed from 21 Tory MPs who had voted against his Government. Among those effectively kicked out of the party in this manner were two former Chancellors, eight ex-Cabinet

---

1 'Boris Johnson asks Queen to suspend parliament,' by Jessica Elgot and Heather Stewart, 28 August 2019, theguardian.com.

2 'Parliament suspension: Thousands protest across the UK,' 31 August 2019, bbc.com.

ministers, and Winston Churchill's grandson. The expulsions deprived the Government of its parliamentary majority.[3]

As the witching hour for the beginning of the prorogation drew near in the Commons, opposition MPs 'threw themselves at the speaker's chair to keep him from standing up and allowing the chamber to be closed.' Soon thereafter, a panel of three judges in the Court of Session, Scotland's highest court, ruled that Johnson's prorogation had been 'unlawful because it had the purpose of stymying Parliament'. The implication was that Boris had misled the Queen about his motivations for the prorogation, a transgression for which at least one ex-Conservative MP said the Prime Minister should resign.[4]

The Scottish verdict did not end the suspension of Parliament, but it did conflict with a ruling by London's High Court that the judiciary could not pass judgment on the motivations for Johnson's action. Less than two weeks later the Supreme Court stepped in to deliver the final judicial word. In an 'extraordinary rebuke' to the Prime Minister, the court, which up to this point had largely avoided political disputes, unanimously ruled that 'The Prime Minister's advice to Her Majesty was unlawful, void and of no effect.' Parliament, therefore, was no longer suspended. Speaker John Bercow later announced that the Commons would convene of the following day. Meanwhile Boris, who at the time was meeting with President Trump at the United Nations, stated that while he 'profoundly' disagreed with the Supreme Court's ruling, 'we respect the judiciary in our country, we respect the court.'[5]

3 'Twenty-one Tory rebels lose party whip after backing bid to block no-deal Brexit,' by Anahita Houssein-Pour, 4 September 2019, politicshome.com.
4 *The New York Times*, 12 September 2019, p. A8.
5 *The New York Times*, 25 September 2019, p. 1.

94. BORIS PURGES MODERATE TORIES

As it became clear that Theresa May soon would be forced to resign as Conservative leader, many of the party's moderates began to hope that by backing Boris to replace her, they would be able to take control of the party from hard-line Brexiteers. To be sure, Johnson had been a leading champion of Brexit. But earlier, as mayor of London, he had been considerably more centrist and pragmatic. So some moderates calculated that if they supported Boris, who seemed likely to win the leadership in any event, they could obtain in return key posts in his administration, and with them a chance to shape his views in a more centrist direction.[1]

Around the same time, concerned about the increasingly hard-line statements of Johnson and other leadership candidates, a number of senior Tories, led by Chancellor Philip Hammond, publicly warned that moderates in the party might be willing to bring down the Prime Minister, and trigger a general election, if the latter sought to pursue a no-deal Brexit without parliamentary permission. Hammond implied that he was himself willing to risk expulsion from the party by voting against his own Prime Minister in a confidence motion.[2]

Moderates were soon disabused of any illusion that they might be able to rein in Johnson. Soon after becoming Prime Minister in July 2019 Boris launched what a Tory MP characterised as 'not so much a reshuffle as a summer's day massacre'. Seventeen senior ministers from the previous Government were sacked or resigned, including a 'Gaukeward Squad' of four of May's cabinet colleagues (including Justice Secretary David Gauke), who quit to preserve their freedom to oppose a no-deal Brexit. Many of those purged had backed the leadership bid of Jeremy Hunt, the former Foreign Secretary, who declined a post in the

---

1 'Conservative moderates plan to take back control of Boris Johnson as Prime Minister,' by Adam Payne and Adam Bienkov, 23 May 2019, businessinsider. com.

2 'Brexit: top Tories would bring down any PM who backs no deal,' by Rowena Mason, 26 May 2019, theguardian.com.

new administration. Such a major purge of senior Tories was virtually unprecedented and was thought to make it less likely that Johnson's Government would long survive.[3]

The implosion of Johnson's Government seemed all the more likely after Boris announced plans to prorogue Parliament, unlawfully as it turned out. On 3 September, while Johnson was addressing the Commons, Phillip Lee dramatically left the Tory benches to sit with the Liberal Democrats, transforming Boris into the first leader of a minority government since 1996. Lee later accused the Government of 'aggressively pursuing a damaging Brexit in unprincipled ways' and the Conservatives of having 'become infected with the twin diseases of populism and English nationalism'.[4]

Later that day, 21 Tory MPs had the whip removed after they supported an opposition effort to prevent a no-deal Brexit. Among those effectively expelled from the party were Hammond and Kenneth Clarke, another ex-chancellor, as well as Sir Nicholas Soames, the grandson of Sir Winston Churchill.[5] (In late October, the whip was restored to 10 of the rebels, but not Hammond or Clarke. Of the 10, four, Soames among them, previously had announced they would stand down in the next election.[6])

Two days later, Jo Johnson, Boris's younger brother, announced his resignation as Business Minister and MP, indicating that he was 'torn between family loyalty and the national interest'.[7]

Soon thereafter Work and Pensions Secretary Amber Rudd quit both the cabinet and the Tory party, accusing Johnson of 'political vandalism' for ousting the 21 rebels.[8]

---

3 '"Summer's day massacre" may spell backbench trouble for Boris Johnson,' by Rajeev Syal, 24 July 2019, theguardian.com.

4 'Boris Johnson loses majority as Tory MP Phillip Lee crosses floor to join Lib Dems,' by Rob Merrick, 3 September 2019, independent.co.uk.

5 'Twenty-one Tory rebels lose party whip after backing bid to block no-deal Brexit,' by Anahita Hossein-Pour, 4 September 2019, politicshome.com.

6 'Tories restore party whip to 10 MPs who sought to block no-deal Brexit,' by Peter Walker, 29 October 2019, theguardian.com.

7 'PM's brother quits as Tory MP and minister,' 5 September 2019, bbc.com.

8 'Amber Rudd quits cabinet and attacks PM for "political vandalism"', by Toby Helm, Michael Savage, Andrew Rawnsley and Daniel Boffey, 7 September 2019, theguardian.com.

95. BORIS REQUESTED BREXIT EXTENSION

In March 2017 Theresa May's Government invoked Article 50 of the European Union Treaty. This gave Britain two years to negotiate the terms under which it would leave the EU or be forced to depart without a deal. Parliament repeatedly rejected the settlements May had negotiated, but such was the fear of a no-deal Brexit that it also called on her to ask the EU to extend the deadline, which eventually was set for 31 October 2019. This upset many Brexit supporters, for whom departure without a deal was preferable to seemingly interminable delays. So when Johnson began campaigning to replace May, he pledged that UK would leave the EU by the deadline, 'do or die, come what may'.[1]

The prospects of a no-deal Brexit alarmed many MPs, including some on the Conservative benches. In an apparent attempt to hinder them from tying his hands, Johnson asked the Queen to suspend Parliament soon after he became Prime Minister. This did not prevent the Commons from passing (with the support of 21 Tory rebels) a Bill requiring that the Prime Minister seek an extension of the deadline if he did not receive parliamentary approval for either an EU withdrawal agreement or no-deal Brexit by 19 October. The legislation came to be known as the Benn Act.[2]

The following day, after the Commons had rejected his attempt to call an early election, Boris stated that he would 'rather be dead in a ditch' than ask for another extension, although he declined to indicate whether he would resign if Parliament forced him to make such a request.[3]

A few days later there were reports that Johnson was considering a plan to 'sabotage' Parliament's efforts by sending the EU both a letter requesting an extension and another

---

1 'Boris Johnson makes "do or die" commitment to Brexit by Oct 21 as he hits campaign trail,' by Michael Settle, 25 June 2019, heraldscotland.com.

2 'Brexit: MPs back Bill aimed at blocking no deal,' 4 September 2019, bbc.com.

3 'Boris Johnson: I'd rather be dead in a ditch than agree Brexit extension,' by Kate Proctor and Peter Walker, 5 September 2019, theguardian.com.

indicating that the Government did not really want one. Senior judges and lawyers indicated that such a scheme would put Boris in contempt of court. Lord Macdonald, former Director of Public Prosecutions, said 'This is the sort of disreputable wheeze that might appeal to an advisor in Downing Street, but is unlikely to appeal to a court. The predictable result would be an injunction requiring the Prime Minister to do what should be first nature to him: obey the law.'[4] There were even calls for Parliament to impeach Johnson if he tried to thwart the law preventing a no-deal Brexit, a sanction Boris himself had sought against Tony Blair.[5]

Johnson subsequently negotiated his own withdrawal deal with the EU, but when he brought it before Parliament MPs supported a move to withhold approval until after the passage of legislation to implement it. Despite losing this crucial vote at the eleventh hour, Boris promised to press on 'undaunted' for Brexit on 31 October.[6]

In the end, Johnson sent the EU three letters. The first was an unsigned photocopy of the request the Benn Act obliged him to make, seeking an extension until 31 January 2020. The second was an explanatory missive from the UK's ambassador to the EU. And the third was a personal message, signed by Boris, explaining why he did not actually want the extension. This approach was not only 'clearly against the spirit of the Benn Act', according to a former Tory minister, but also could 'put government law officers in a very uncomfortable position' given that Downing Street apparently had the Scottish court's assurances that it would not employ this sort of shenanigans.[7]

---

4 'Boris Johnson "sabotage" letter to EU "would break law,"' by Aamna Mohdin, 9 September 2019, theguardian.com.
5 'Brexit extension: "Impeach Boris Johnson if law ignored"', 9 September 2019, bbc.com.
6 'Brexit: Johnson vows to press on despite defeat over deal delay,' 19 October 2019, bbc.com.
7 'Brexit: Johnson sends unsigned letter asking for delay, and second arguing against it,' by Daniel Boffey, 20 October 2019, theguardian.com.

96. BORIS CHANGES MIND ON IRISH BORDER

In the run-up to the 2016 referendum, various claims were made about how the UK's departure from the EU could affect the border between Northern Ireland and the Republic of Ireland. Chancellor George Osborne averred, 'There would have to be a hardening of the border,' imposed by either the British or Irish government. This would mark a return to the situation during the Troubles, when checkpoints were established between Ulster and the Republic. Johnson (and others) argued by contrast that arrangements on the Irish border would remain 'absolutely unchanged' by Brexit, with the same freedom of travel between the two territories as had existed for almost a century. This ignored the fact that the UK and the Republic joined the EU on the same day, meaning that Brexit would mark the first time that one was in while the other was out.[1]

In the wake of the vote to Leave the EU, Prime Minister Theresa May sought to negotiate a departure agreement that would avoid creating a hard Irish border, in part because the reintroduction of customs checks could jeopardise the peace settlement that ended the Troubles. However, in February 2018, Johnson wrote her a letter claiming it was 'wrong to see the task as maintaining "no border"'. Instead the government should focus on stopping the border from 'becoming significantly harder'. Some border checks, he implied, would not be very problematic: 'Even if a hard border is reintroduced, we would expect to see 95%+ of goods pass the border (without) checks.' Former Conservative minister Michael Heseltine characterised Johnson's missive as displaying 'the most remarkable level of duplicity'. The letter's contents were revealed the same day Boris drew ridicule for suggesting that the same technological innovations that obviated borders between London's boroughs

---

1 'Reality Check: Would Brexit mean border controls for NI?' 7 June 2016, bbc.com.

could be used to finesse Irish border checks. When questioned whether traveling within a city really was analogous to international trade, Johnson insisted that he had made 'a very relevant comparison'. But Labour MP David Lammy, who represented a London constituency, called Johnson's parallel 'not only rank stupidity, it is ignorant and wilfully reckless.'[2]

Several months later, however, Johnson derided the border issue as 'a gnat' while referring to the 'backstop', the mechanism by which negotiators had tried to avoid the creation of customs checkpoints through the development of technological innovations, as a 'monstrosity'. Given that the technology to monitor accurately trade between Northern Ireland and the Republic of Ireland without such checkpoints did not yet exist, the backstop required that Ulster remain part of the EU customs union until the necessary technology was developed. Treating Northern Ireland differently from the rest of the United Kingdom was, according to Johnson, a 'constitutional abomination'. And the backstop 'is little short of an attempt to annex Northern Ireland. It would imply customs and regulatory controls between Britain and Northern Ireland, and therefore a border down the Irish sea.'[3]

A year later, Boris had replaced May as Prime Minister, partly due to complaints about the backstop. Johnson then negotiated a deal with Brussels that took the entire UK out of the EU customs union. However, goods shipped to Belfast from the rest of the UK would be subject to EU duties if they possibly could be transported onward to the Republic of Ireland. Effectively, 'the customs border will be across the sea between Britain and Northern Ireland.'[4]

---

2 'New Boris Johnson comments on post-Brexit Irish border cause stir,' 28 February 2018, euractiv.com.
3 'Boris Johnson: Irish Border problem a "gnat" and backstop a "monstrosity",' by Marie O'Halloran, 16 September 2018, irishtimes.com.
4 'What is happening in Brexit? The defeat of Boris Johnson's timetable and what happens next,' by Adam Taylor, 22 October 2019, washingtonpost.com.

97. BORIS CALLS AN EARLY ELECTION, ON FOURTH TRY

In response to legislative defeats in late 2019, Prime Minister Johnson repeatedly sought to call an early general election, only to be thwarted by the Fixed-Term Parliaments Act (2011), which mandated that such a motion receive the support of two-thirds of the entire Commons membership. On 4 September, after the Commons twice defeated the Government by supporting a Bill that would ban a no-deal Brexit, Boris unsuccessfully sought an early election. Five days later, on the day Parliament was to be prorogued, he tried again, with similar results. And on 28 October, days before the deadline by which he had pledged to achieve Brexit, he again sought an early general election. This time his call received 299 votes, slightly more than his previous efforts but still well short of the 434 votes required.[1]

But once the EU granted an extension of the Brexit deadline from 31 October to 31 January 2020, and thereby temporarily ended the possibility that the UK would depart without a deal, the primary Labour objection to an early poll disappeared. So, on 29 October, Johnson proposed a Bill that would set aside the Fixed-Term Parliaments Act and authorise an election on 12 December. Ironically, the Commons approved this legislation by a vote of 438 to 20, meaning that it actually had the super-majority required under the Act. Opposition parties had sought a slightly earlier election 'to cut off any possibility that Mr Johnson could make a fresh attempt to ram through his Brexit deal before Parliament is dissolved.'[2]

---

1 'Boris Johnson fails in third attempt to call early general election,' by Rowena Mason, 28 October 2019, theguardian.com.
2 'Boris Johnson one step closer to a general election after MPs approve December 12 date,' by Robert Peston, 29 October 2019, itv.com.

98. BORIS WINS BIG IN 2019 GENERAL ELECTION

When Johnson finally persuaded Parliament to call a general election, he had reasons for optimism about its outcome. Polls showed his Tories with a double-digit lead over Labour, whose head, Jeremy Corbin, was the most unpopular opposition leader in decades. And where Labour attitudes toward Europe were complicated, Boris's electoral message was simple: 'Let's get Brexit done,' that is, push through Parliament the deal he already had negotiated with the EU. Still, a snap election was not without risks. For one, Johnson's message was likely to attract some traditional Labour supporters but alienate others who previously had voted Tory. Add in an increasingly volatile electorate, more opportunities for tactical voting and Nigel Farage's new Brexit Party and the difficulty of predicting the election's outcome with any confidence grew exponentially. Plus, it was not beyond the realm of possibility that voters, long weary of the endless debate about Brexit, might pick their candidates on some other basis, such as support for increased public services, to the detriment of the Tories, who had long supported austerity. Finally, there was recent history: Theresa May began the 2017 election campaign with an even bigger lead than Boris's but ended up losing her majority. Although the charismatic and popular Johnson was expected to campaign better than May, calling an early election was a 'big gamble'.[1]

It was not just a risk for the Tories. Boris won his Uxbridge and South Ruislip constituency by 5,034 votes in 2017. This meant that he would defend a smaller majority than any sitting Prime Minister in almost a century, with a 'real risk' he would lose his seat.[2] Indeed, three weeks before the vote the betting

1 'Boris Johnson gets his Christmas election,' 29 October 2019, economist. com.
2 'What happens if Boris Johnson loses his seat?' by Rebecca Speare-Cole, 11 December 2019, standard.co.uk.

firm Ladbrokes indicated there was a better than one-in-five (22 per cent) chance that Johnson would not be returned.[3]

In the days immediately following Parliament's dissolution, the dangers were apparent, for Boris 'seemed at times unsure, tone deaf and gaffe prone' rather than the 'ace campaigner' many had expected. He was confronted by angry citizens, in one case cancelling a visit to a Glastonbury bakery to avoid climate-change protesters. He told Ulster manufacturers that if they were asked to fill out extra paperwork to ship goods to Britain as a result of his Brexit deal, 'I will direct them to throw that form in the bin,' even though his own government has indicated that exporters will have to submit 'exit summary declarations'.[4]

Perhaps because of these stumbles, Boris soon began attracting comments less for what he did than for what he did not do: submit to interviews. He refused to commit to an interview with Andrew Neil of the BBC, even though all the leaders of the other main parties had undergone such an interrogation. He similarly was the only leader to decline an interview with ITV's Julie Etchingham. He also skipped Channel 4's climate debate, where he was replaced by a melting ice sculpture, and a head-to-head debate with Corbyn.[5] And, most memorably, Johnson was reported to have hidden in a walk-in refrigerator to avoid an interview with Piers Morgan, who accosted the Prime Minister during an early-morning visit to a dairy. This incident came two days after Boris put a journalist's phone in his pocket during an interview rather than look at a picture of a young boy asleep on a Leeds hospital floor.[6]

Despite, or perhaps because of, Johnson's antics the Conservatives won their biggest majority since 1987.[7]

3 'Boris Johnson Has 22% Chance of Losing Seat, Bookmaker Says,' by Dara Doyle, 22 November 2019, bloomberg.com.

4 'Boris Johnson Was Supposed to Be an Ace Campaigner. So Why is He Stumbling?' by Mark Landler and Stephen Castle, 14 November 2019, nytimes.com.

5 'BBC's Andrew Neil lays down gauntlet to Boris Johnson over interview,' by Nadeem Badshah, 5 December 2019, theguardian.com.

6 'Boris Johnson "hides in fridge" to avoid Piers Morgan interview,' by Heather Stewart and Aamna Mohdin, 11 December 2019, theguardian.com.

7 'Election results 2019: Boris Johnson returns to power with big majority,' 13 December 2019, bbc.com.

99. BORIS 'GETS BREXIT DONE,' RIGHT?

In the end it was something of an anti-climax. After whinging about Europe for most of the nearly five decades the coutnry had been formally tied to it and discussing divorce to the exclusion of pretty much everything else for more than three years, Britain finally left the EU at midnight on 31 January, Brussels time. Prime Minister Boris Johnson could claim, with some justification, that he had fulfilled his promise to the voters who recently had given him a large parliamentary majority in order to 'get Brexit done.'

But while Britain has formally left the EU, it largely would behave, and be treated, as if it was still a member of the bloc until the end of 2020. In the interim, Johnson would seek to negotiate the country's future commercial relationship with Europe. Although he repeatedly indicated that he would not seek an extension of the trade-agreement deadline past 31 December 2020, there was widespread scepticism that such a complicated deal could be worked out in such a short period (particularly after the disruptions caused by the outbreak of the COVID-19 virus in early 2020). In any case, Boris would face some difficult choices. Many who supported him in southern England envision a post-Brexit Britain that features a leaner, less regulated State, a 'Singapore on the Thames'. But former Labour supporters in northern England often backed Brexit in the hopes that it would lead to an increase in spending on the NHS and other public services. Moreover, European leaders have made clear that the further Britain deviates from EU labour, product safety and environmental standards, the greater the price it will have to pay to get access to their market, which accounts for almost half of the UK's exports. Much of Brexit, in short, remains undone.[1]

---

1 'Brexit Is Finally Happening. Now Things Are Going to Get Really Complicated.' By Peter S. Goodman, 31 January 2020, The New York Times, p. B1.

100. BORIS JOHNSON'S RISE WAS LARGELY BUILT ON LIES

Some readers will no doubt have noticed an existential paradox in the preceding pages: this is a book of facts about a man whose commitment to the truth, to empirical reality, to facts, is at best contingent. Occasionally his dishonesty has had a detrimental effect on his career: he has been fired from positions in both journalism and politics for failing to tell the truth. But mostly dissimilation has worked out well for Boris, powering his ascent to supreme political office. The man who brought you Boris Bikes and Boris Buses has thrived through the propagation of Boris Facts, nuggets of verisimilitude rather than veracity. Indeed, it is safe to say that you are reading this book about facts about Boris precisely because of his cavalier attitude toward facts.

Johnson fascinates partly because he seems a 16-stone id run amok, a man so in the thrall of his passions that he cannot prevent himself from doing awkward, embarrassing or inappropriate things. Chaos, chagrin and hilarity ensue. But this image is largely contrived, cultivated not only for comedic effect and attention but also because it provides protection. How can a shambolic clown be taken seriously? And if he is not taken seriously, how can he be held accountable? Perhaps Johnson's greatest accomplishment has been to create a public persona impervious to the scandals that would doom lesser mortals, for outlandish behaviour is baked into the package.

That Johnson gets away with so many untruths is perhaps less surprising than the nature of his misrepresentations. It is not uncommon for people to lie to make themselves seem better or more respectable. Boris does this, but also, the reverse. Thus he infamously has referred to Africans as 'flag-waving piccaninnies' with 'watermelon smiles'. He has characterised homosexuals as 'tank-topped bumboys'. And has opined that women in burkas looked like 'letter boxes' and 'bank robbers'. His questionable comments about women have been frequent.[1]

Yet those who know him best do not believe Johnson is racist, homophobic or Islamophobic. (Sexist is another matter.) Sonia Purnell, a biographer and former colleague, writes that Johnson demonstrated from a young age 'a genuine empathy for outsiders of whatever national or racial origin'. She notes that unlike many at Eton, he did not ignore classmates from ethnic minorities. And while campaigning for mayor of London, Boris extolled his Muslim Turkish immigrant roots.[2]

If, as it seems, Boris is not really a bigot, why does he occasionally say and do things that suggest that he is? By acting a bit naughty or edgy Boris appears to be trying to ingratiate himself to those who do subscribe to those abhorrent views. But since he is pretending to be a clown while also hinting at being a bigot, Boris can portray any offensiveness as irony misunderstood by his critics. By saying politically incorrect things while denying that he really means them, Boris is, as always, seeking to have his cake and eat it too. As he admitted in 2000, he was 'A wise guy playing the fool to win'.[3]

On Europe, the same process has been at work in spades. Despite having lived in Brussels, being the son of an MEP, and knowing many of the major players, Boris opted to pander to Middle England prejudices. He thus portrayed European Union officials as bumbling buffoons, without, of course the charm he imbued in his own Bertie-Wooster shtick. By peddling the dubious notion that these incompetent and humourless bureaucrats were intent on squeezing all the fun out of Britain, like Dementors in a Harry Potter novel, Johnson made a name for himself but at the cost of exacerbating divisions within

---

1 'Boris Johnson called gay men "tank-topped bumboys" and black people "piccaninnies" with "watermelon smiles",' by Adam Bienkov, 22 November 2019, businessinsider.com.

2 Purnell, pp. 42, 55, 340.

3 Vasudevan, A., 'The Thinking Man's Idiot: The Wit and Wisdom of Boris Johnson, (London: New Holland Publishers, 2008), p. 9.

both the Conservative Party and British society. Later, having translated his popular appeal into public office, Boris dished out more untruths about Europe to propel himself to the pinnacle of political power. Again, those who know him insist that Boris did not really believe what he said about Europe but instead humorously purveyed falsehoods to draw attention to himself and further his career.[4]

It is far from clear that Boris Johnson, the product of Britain's finest schools, a man of considerable intellect, talent and wit, not to mention extraordinary charisma, needed to lie to achieve journalistic and political success. What does seem obvious is that the little boy who dreamed of becoming 'world king' has come rather close to realising his ambitions. Shortly after the 2019 General Election *The Economist* dubbed him 'King Boris' noting that his large parliamentary majority left him 'well placed to become one of the most powerful Prime Ministers in modern times'. Johnson was thought poised to preside not only over Britain's renegotiation of its relationship with the outside world but also over the reconstitution of the country's party system as he sought to use increased public spending to bring into the Tory tent many from the Midlands and North of England who traditionally had supported Labour.[5] Whatever one thinks of the man himself, this surely represents a triumph for Boris. It's a fact.

---

4 Gimson, pp. xiv–xv, 98–103.
5 'Bagehot: One nation under Boris,' *The Economist* (US edition), 4 January 2020, p. 41.